THE
QUILT BLOCK
COOKBOOK

THE
QUILT BLOCK
COOKBOOK

50 BLOCK RECIPES, 7 SAMPLER QUILTS, ENDLESS POSSIBILITIES

AMY GIBSON

Published in 2016 by Lucky Spool Media, LLC
www.luckyspool.com
info@luckyspool.com

Text © Amy Gibson
Editor Susanne Woods
Designer Rae Ann Spitzenberger
Illustrations Kari Vojtechovsky

Photographs pages 4-5, 8, 15, 146 © Lauren Hunt

Photographs pages 2-3, 11, 160 © Amy Gibson

All other photography © Page + Pixel, LLC

9 8 7 6 5 4 3 2 1

First Edition
Printed in China

Library of Congress Cataloging-in-Publication
Data available upon request

ISBN 978-1-940655-14-7

LSID0032

*To my mother, who took
me to the library.*

CONTENTS

THE BLOCKS

3x3

4x4

5x5

6x6

Staples

THE QUILTS

INTRODUCTION

WHY I HEART BLOCKS

Quilt blocks. We collect them, we swap them, we join clubs and classes to make them. We tape them to our walls, stack them on our shelves, post pictures of them online, and, yes, stitch them into quilts. From bursting blooms to serious squares, quilt blocks are a quilter's trading cards. They're our Friday night fix, our one-at-a-time victories, our miniature masterpieces. Whether we're pooling them to make a community quilt, or just whipping up that perfect pop-of-color pillow for the couch, blocks have been, and continue to be a quilting staple.

I see fabric trends come and go like summer storms, and piecing styles endlessly evolving, but the square by square tradition of my mother's mother's mother is here to stay, and it's easy to see why. There's a reason that this old-as-the-hills approach to patchwork continues to beckon quilters of all aesthetics again and again.

First, quilt blocks are incredibly versatile. It never ceases to amaze me at how much punch you can pack into a 12" square. I adore design play, and blocks are the perfect canvas for it,

but I think what I love about them even more, is that they're just plain approachable, and for some of us, the idea of building a quilt, block by block, just feels, well...good. I love making lists, hanging my clothes by color, and cleaning my house room by room, so it's no wonder I love block-based quilts. In my order-craving mind, they just make sense. I might not have time to clean my whole house, but I can clean one room, and by golly I'll sit in that room and enjoy it—my oasis of order in a sea of chaos. For me, stitching up a single block is a wonderful little triumph. I may have a zillion more to make, and it might be the only sewing I get in that day or week, but in that moment, one block is enough.

And if the block is a miss? Good news! It's not a whole quilt. Blocks are a low commitment, so

Food for Thought

Quilt blocks are like a box of chocolates. Each one is a mini-euphoria—unless you get the one that's filled with toothpaste, in which case you can be thankful the experience is short-lived.

whether the verdict is "in love!" or "not-my-fav", I'm quickly moving on to the next great thing.

So I embrace blocks—I celebrate them for the little wonders they are. But just because they feel comfortable and satisfying to me, doesn't necessarily mean I'm content to throw them into tired, predictable samplers and call it good. For me, the fun lies not only in cooking up fresh, new designs, but also in dreaming up fun and exciting ways to use my quilt blocks. This book offers 7 innovative sampler quilt layouts to dig into. Use up orphan blocks loitering around your sewing room, or stitch up a fresh new batch of beauties to plug into one of my playful, modern layouts (see page 124).

I'll be honest—as much as I adore samplers, sometimes I'm just not in the mood for them, and if that's you right now, don't miss "Beyond the Sampler" (see page 145). We'll dig into getting more from your blocks and creating dynamic design repeats by tapping into the limitless possibilities of 1 and 2-block based quilts. There's a whole lot more to blocks than just samplers!

SHARE THE LOVE

Let's face it. Quilting isn't just about sewing. It's also about community, and when it comes to this community, there can never be enough cooks in the kitchen. What makes quilters unique isn't just the fact that we love to make patchwork, but that we love to come together over our love for making patchwork. So whether it's your first block ever, or your thousandth, don't forget to snap a pic, and show the world what you've cooked up with #TheQuiltBlockCookbook so we can all share the love!

HOW TO USE THIS BOOK

FIT TO SIZE

All of the blocks in this book measure 12 inches *finished*, meaning they measure 12 inches after they've been stitched into a quilt (or 12½ inches including the seam allowances). They each consist of a square grid layout, ranging from a 3x3, all the way up to a 6x6. While there are many other types of block layouts that exist beyond this traditional grid style, I specifically chose to stick to these types of blocks, so that customizing them to suit your tastes would be a cinch. The blocks are conveniently organized in groups of like-sized grid layouts, so you can easily plug units from one block, into another within the same section. Or you can take advantage of the convenient unit-sizing charts (see page 165), and start cooking up your own unique block designs.

The sampler quilts (see page 124) are each specifically sized to fit 12 inch blocks, so you can plug in any of the blocks from this book, or from elsewhere. In fact you may already have a stack of 12 inch blocks hanging out on your shelf, just begging to be used. 12 inch blocks are a very common size, and for good reason. They're divisible by 2, 3, 4, and 6, which makes them incredibly versatile and simple to both design and work with.

KEEP IT SIMPLE

Construction Techniques (see page 149) is your go-to chapter for step-by-step visuals on stitching up all of the units contained in these 50 blocks. While there are often many different ways to construct the same unit, for the purposes of this book, I've employed consistent techniques throughout for the sake of ease and clarity. For

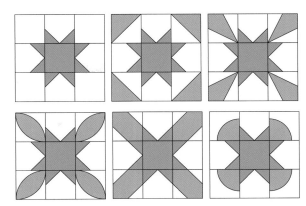

The corners of a block are one of the easiest spots to make a high-impact change to a design.

example, wherever the "stitch & flip" or "drawn line" (see page 149) method can be applied, it has been. Refer back to the Construction Techniques chapter as needed, though after you've jumped in and started stitching up some of the different unit types (like half-square triangles or diamond-in-a-square) you're likely to get more comfortable with them and the need to refer back will become less frequent.

TEMPLATES

Some of the blocks are foundation pieced or contain curved piecing or fusible appliqué , so require paper templates. All of the templates can be found beginning on page 168. Following the instructions in the recipes, and on the templates themselves, photocopy them onto standard 20# copy paper and cut. While the curved unit templates (E1-F5) *do* already include the necessary seam allowances, the foundation paper pieced templates (A-C) do not, so ¼" seam allowances will need to be added to all sides during trimming. The petals (D1-D5) will be fused and then raw edge appliquéd, so they do not need seam allowances.

SEASON TO TASTE

One of the goals in writing this book is for you to feel confident about customizing and adjusting the designs to fit your personal taste. After all, you'll be the one stitching and using these blocks, so I want them to fit your preferences! From fabric choices, to unit styles and methods, by all means, please make these your own. And this is where the unit substitutions come in. Maybe you don't enjoy curves and you don't want them in your block. No problem—use a different unit in those spots. Or maybe your printer is on the fritz and you'd rather not deal with templates. No worries—there are loads of other units that you could add to your block instead. That's the thing about recipes—they make excellent guidelines, but even really delicious recipes tell you to "Season to Taste."

WORKING THE GRID

Here's a quick overview on how grid-style blocks work, and how the grid can be manipulated to achieve a particular design.

A 3x3 unit block is a block in which the geometry has been divided into 3 equally sized units on all sides (so 9 units total). Sometimes it can help to imagine the block on graph paper, where each unit takes up a single square.

Grid style blocks are especially straightforward to work with because the assembly process for stitching the units together into the finished block, is consistent. The units are first stitched into rows, and then the rows are joined on the long side to complete the block.

All of the blocks in this book can be assembled in horizontal rows, except for Block 7, "To & Fro", which is assembled as vertical columns.

Before joining the rows, seams between the units should either be pressed to the side in alternating directions, or open, depending on the specific piecing in the block and your pressing preferences (see Game Plan: A Look at Seam Pressing Strategies on page 160 for more information about pressing seams). Regardless of which direction you press your seams, the seam intersections should be carefully aligned and pinned before joining the rows.

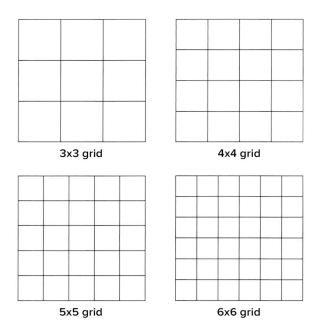

3x3 grid   4x4 grid

5x5 grid   6x6 grid

COMBINING UNITS

Whenever possible, units may be combined to reduce the number of seams in a block. So, for example, in Block 28, "Second Star" (a 4x4 block), instead of using two half-square triangle units for each pair of star points, we can combine that pair into a single unit with the same geometry—a flying geese block (see page. 153). Now, this isn't to say you *must* always combine units. By all means, stitch your blocks in the way that feels most comfortable and pleasing to you, but just keep in mind that combining units can often save you time,

and give your block a cleaner look. Combining units does not change the grid classification of a block. So, the "Second Star" block (see page 76) is still considered a 4x4 block, even though there are areas of it in which two units have been combined into one.

In Block 32, "Flag Day" (see page 84), we see this concept taken even further, where a 2x2 section of the block (4 grid spaces) has been combined into one single unit. This block is still a 5x5, even though units in some areas of the block have been combined to create the desired look.

The "Second Star" Block has a 4x4 grid in which 2 grid units have been combined into a single unit.

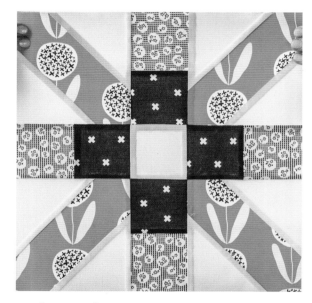

The "Flag Day " block has a 5x5 grid in which 4 units have been combined into a single unit.

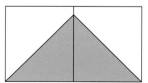 

2 Half-square triangle units vs. a single flying geese unit

DIVIDING UNITS

In the same way that units can be combined, they can also be divided. You may notice some blocks contain what appears to be a grid within a grid. We see this in "Sugarplum" (see page 64), where the perimeter units are clearly arranged in a 4x4 grid, but the units in the center of the block are smaller, appearing not to fit into this sized grid. These units have been divided into quarters. Still the same grid—a 4x4 block—but with some of the units on the grid divided into smaller patches.

The "Sugarplum" block has a 4x4 grid in which 4 units in the center have been divided into quarters.

Don't Forget the Seam Allowances

If you choose to play around with combining or dividing unit sections, don't forget to account for the lost or gained seam allowances, which are always ¼" per raw edge, or ½" total per piece.

THE PINK OF PERFECTION

Once you've whipped up your blocks, there's just one more step before they're ready to be stitched into a quilt. "Squaring up" completed, pressed blocks is that final trim around the perimeter of the block to make sure it's perfectly sized and that the edges are neat and clean. Even with accurate cutting, seam allowances, and proper pressing, most blocks will still need to be squared up, however minimal the excess may be. After all, who doesn't love pieces that fit together perfectly?

All of the blocks in this book should be pressed well, and then squared to 12½". While you can use any sized square ruler that is larger than your squaring up size, using a ruler that fits the size precisely makes this step quick and easy. So, I recommend you use a 12½" ruler for squaring up all of the blocks in this book, as well as any other blocks you may want to plug into the samplers (see page 17 for more information about quilting rulers).

STOCKING YOUR KITCHEN

Fabulous patchwork starts with having the right tools at the ready. Help make your process more efficient and enjoyable by investing in the right tools for the job.

¼″ Patchwork Foot

A ¼" presser foot, also sometimes called a patchwork foot or a piecing foot, can be a great help for stitching accurate ¼" seams quickly and easily.

Self-Healing Cutting Mats

Look for a mat no smaller than 18" x 24", and if you can go larger, do it. Take care to store your mat in a flat position, and to keep heat sources away from it, including your iron, laptop, hot mugs or plates. Heat can permanently warp or distort the mat.

Rotary Cutters

A 45mm blade is standard for most fabric cutting. For smaller patches or curves, a 28mm cutter provides additional control. Larger 60mm cutters work well for trimming thicker layers.

Rulers

Clear acrylic quilting rulers come in a wide variety of shapes and sizes. Great sizes to start with are the 6½" x 24", which is perfect for cutting strips of yardage; as well as the 12½" square which is ideal for squaring up blocks. The 4½" comes in handy for trimming units.

Tape Measure

Long, flexible sewing tape measures come in handy for measuring those extra-long strips, backing fabric pieces, and even the size of your finished quilt.

Straight Pins

Flat head flower pins are easy to grasp and they lie flat on fabric, minimizing puckering or bumps.

They're also long and thin, slipping in and out of the fabric easily without leaving noticeable holes.

Fabric Glue Stick

Washable fabric glue can be used in various places throughout the piecing process. Fabric glue sticks are especially helpful in techniques like foundation paper piecing and machine appliqué to temporarily keep templates and patches in place.

Scissors

Although most of the cutting we do in quilting is with the rotary cutter, quality fabric scissors are helpful for everything from snipping threads to trimming away excess batting. Invest in a quality pair of large fabric shears for the bigger jobs, and a smaller pair of sharp-point sewing scissors for detailed trimming or snipping.

Tracing Wheel

This sewing tool is typically used for garment making, but it's also a perfect way to perforate paper templates during foundation paper piecing.

Seam Ripper

Loathed and loved, the seam ripper is an essential for even the most seasoned quilters. Look for one with a sharp point, an easy-to-hold handle, and a safety cap.

Safety Pins

Safety pins can be used to baste the layers of a quilt together so they don't shift around when you add the quilting stitches. Look for 1½" (size 2) nickel-plated steel pins with a curved shape that makes for easier handling during basting.

INGREDIENTS

BASIC TRIANGLES
From simple to fancy, half- and quarter-square triangle unit variations do the heavy lifting in many blocks.

CORNER CUTTERS
It's all corner work on these diagonal stripe, diamond-in-a-square, and snowball-style units.

SHORT & TALL TRIANGLES
Triangles make the perfect star points, sun beams, arrows & frame corners.

  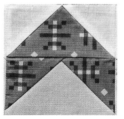  

BURSTS & BLOOMS

From shining diamonds and burst shapes, to soft petals and curves, these units add a pinch of whimsy to your patchwork.

 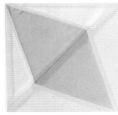   

STRAIGHT AWAYS

Squares and rectangle-based configurations work well as foundations and connectors between flashier units.

   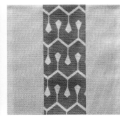 

THE
BLOCKS

Grid: 3x3

(4) flying geese units in red

(4) flying geese units in pink

(1) plain square in red

(4) burst units in green

CUTTING

WHITE FABRIC
(8) 2½" x 4½" rectangles (geese)
(8) 2½" x 5½" rectangles (bursts)

RED FABRIC
(1) 4½" square (plain center)
(8) 2½" squares (geese)

PINK FABRIC
(8) 2½" squares (geese)

GREEN FABRIC
(4) 4¾" squares (bursts)

MAKE IT

1. Make 4 photocopies of Template A at 200% scale (see page 169), then foundation piece (see page 158) 4 green/white burst units.

2. Create 4 red/white and 4 pink/white flying geese (see page 153) for a total of 8 units.

3. Stitch each pink geese unit to a red geese unit along the longer side, so the triangles are facing the same direction. If the white triangles are pointing down, the pink unit will be on top. Press.

4. Assemble the block by stitching 3 rows of 3 units each.

RECIPE

2

CHERRY ON TOP

Grid: 3x3

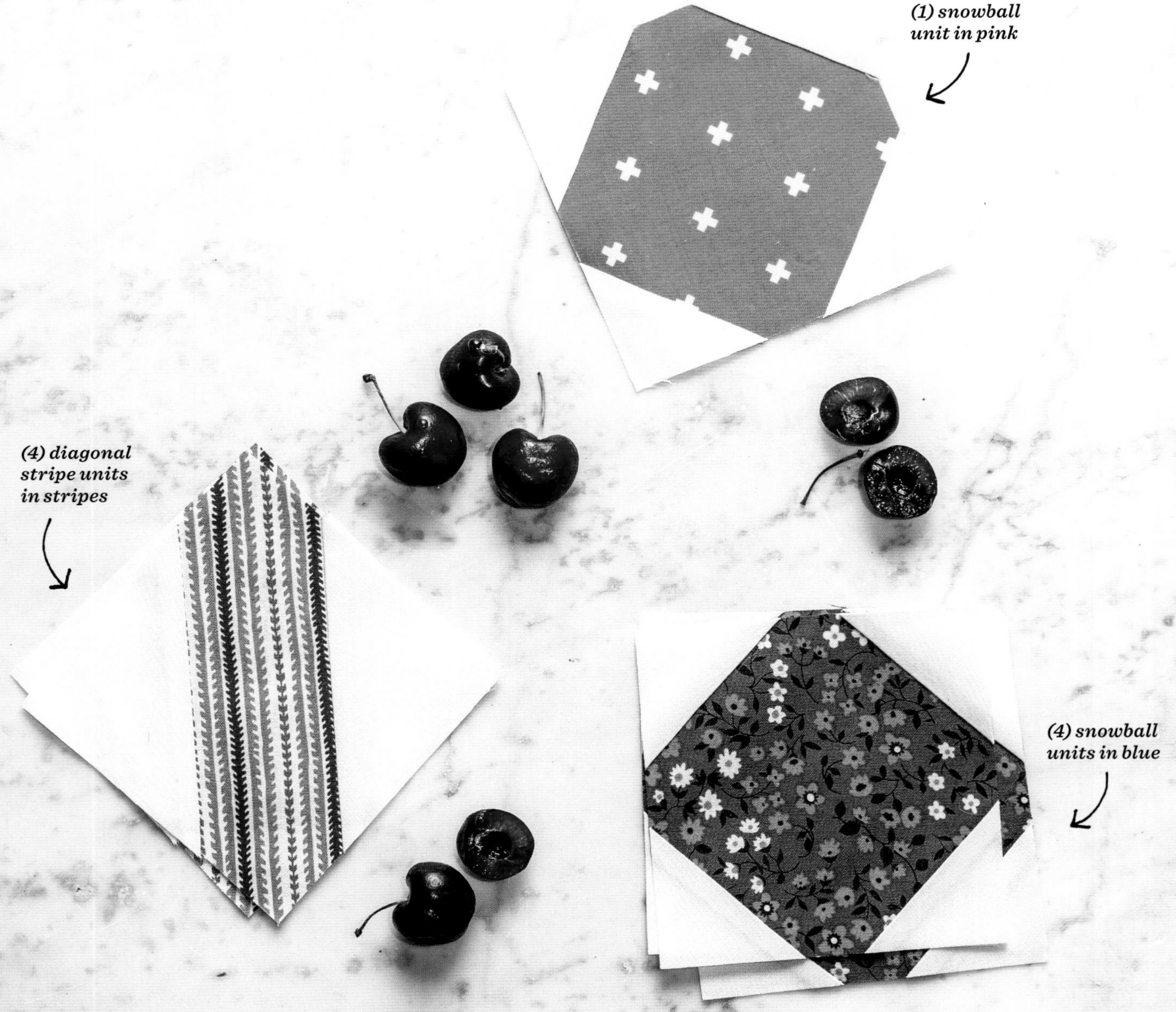
(1) snowball unit in pink
(4) diagonal stripe units in stripes
(4) snowball units in blue

CUTTING

WHITE FABRIC
(20) 1⅞" squares (snowballs)
(8) 3⅛" squares (diagonal stripes)

PINK FABRIC
(1) 4½" square (center snowball)

BLUE FABRIC
(4) 4½" squares (snowballs)

STRIPED FABRIC
(4) 4½" squares (diagonal stripes)

MAKE IT

1. Create 4 blue/white and
1 pink/white snowball units
(see page 157).

2. Create 4 diagonal stripe units
(see page 151). If using a directional
fabric, take care that the direction of
the fabric is aligned in all 4 units.

3. Assemble the block by stitching
3 rows of 3 units each. Press.

LEMON WHIP

Grid: 3x3

(4) quarter-square triangle units in orange and multi

(4) petal units in yellow

(1) diamond-in-a-square unit in large print

CUTTING

WHITE FABRIC
(4) 2½" squares (diamond in squares)
(2) 5¼" squares (QSTs)
(4) 4½" squares (petals)

LARGE PRINT FABRIC
(1) 4½" square (diamond in square)

ORANGE FABRIC
(1) 5¼" square (QST)

MULTI FLORAL FABRIC
(1) 5¼" square (QST)

YELLOW FABRIC
(4) Template D4 (petals)
Double-sided fusible web is bonded to the wrong side of this fabric before the petals are cut.

MAKE IT

1. Photocopy the Template D4 (see page 172). Trace, cut and appliqué (see page 161) 4 yellow fabric petals to the 4½" white squares, centered.

2. Create 4 orange/multi/white QST units (see page 156). The 2-toned units are created when HSTs of 2 different prints are paired.

3. Create 1 print/white diamond-in-a-square unit (see page 152).

4. Assemble the block by stitching 3 rows of 3 units each. Press.

RECIPE

4 | SHINE

Grid: 3x3

(4) diagonal diamond units in aqua

(4) triangle units in purple

(1) plain square in purple

CUTTING

WHITE FABRIC
(16) 5¼" x 2" rectangles (diamonds)
(8) 5½" x 3" rectangles (triangles)

PURPLE FABRIC
(1) 4½" square (plain center)
(4) 5" squares (triangles)

AQUA FABRIC
(8) 4" squares (diamonds)

MAKE IT

1. Make 8 photocopies of Template C at 100% (see page 170) and foundation piece (see page 158) 8 aqua/white diamond units. Stitch pairs of the triangular units together along the longest side to create 4 diagonal diamond units (see page 151). Press seams open.

2. Make 4 photocopies of Template B at 100% (see page 171) and foundation piece (see page 158) 4 purple/white units.

3. Assemble the block by stitching 3 rows of 3 units each. Press.

TRUE NORTH

Grid: 3x3

(1) plain square in green

CUTTING

WHITE FABRIC
(4) 4" squares (half diamonds)
(2) 5½" squares (QSTs)

GREEN FABRIC
(1) 4½" square (plain center)

ORANGE FABRIC
(1) 5½" square (QSTs)
(2) 4⅞" squares (half diamonds)
   Sub-cut in half, diagonally

NAVY FABRIC
(4) 5¼" x 2" rectangles (diagonal diamonds)

GRAY FABRIC
(4) 5¼" x 2" rectangles (diagonal diamonds)

AQUA FABRIC
(1) 5½" square (QSTs)

(4) half-diagonal diamond units in orange, navy & gray

(4) QST units

MAKE IT

1. Make 4 photocopies of Template C at 100% (see page 170) and cut out the templates outside the trim line. Foundation piece (see page 158) the navy, white and gray diamond units. Position the navy in section C2, and gray in section C3. Remove the paper, then stitch each diamond unit to an orange triangle to create 4 squares. Press.

2. Create 4 orange/aqua/white QST units (see page 156). The 2-toned units are created when HSTs of 2 different prints are paired.

3. Assemble the block by stitching 3 rows of 3 units each. Press.

OPEN SESAME

Grid: 3x3

CUTTING

WHITE FABRIC
(1) 4½" square (diamond-in-a-square)
(16) 2½" squares (geese)
(4) 4½" squares (curves)
   subcut into 4 of Template E4

YELLOW FABRIC
(4) 2½" squares (diamond-in-a-square)
(4) 4½" x 2½" rectangles (geese)

PINK FABRIC
(4) 4½" x 2½" rectangles (geese)

NAVY FABRIC
(4) 4" squares (curves)
   subcut into 4 of Template F4

(4) curved units in navy

(4) flying geese units in pink

(4) flying geese units in yellow

(1) diamond-in-a-square unit in yellow

MAKE IT

1. Create 4 yellow/white and 4 pink/white flying geese (see page 153) for a total of 8 units.

2. Stitch each pink goose unit to a yellow goose unit along the longer side, so the triangles are facing the same direction.

3. Create 1 diamond-in-a-square unit (see page 152) using the 4½" white square and remaining yellow squares.

4. Create 4 navy/white curved units (see page 151) using the Templates on page 173.

5. Assemble the block by stitching 3 rows of 3 units each. Press.

TO & FRO

Grid: 3x3

(6) flying geese units in various prints

(6) triangle units in various prints

CUTTING

WHITE FABRIC
(12) 5½" x 3" rectangles (triangles)
(12) 2½" squares (geese)

VARIOUS PRINTS
(6) 5" squares (triangles)
(6) 4½" x 2½" rectangles (geese)

MAKE IT

1. Create 6 flying geese units (see page 153) using the prints and white fabric.

2. Make 6 photocopies of Template B at 100% (see page 171) and foundation piece (see page 158) 6 units using the prints and white.

3. Assemble the block by stitching 3 vertical rows of 4 units each. Press.

STARBOARD

Grid: 3x3

(4) diagonal stripe units in pink and navy

(4) QST units in green

(1) diamond-in-a-square unit in pink

CUTTING

WHITE FABRIC
(4) 2½" squares (diamond)
(2) 5¼" squares (QSTs)
(4) 4½" squares (diagonal stripes)

PINK FABRIC
(1) 4½" square (diamond)
(4) 2½" squares (diagonal stripes)

GREEN FABRIC
(2) 5¼" squares (QSTs)

NAVY FABRIC
(4) 2½" squares (diagonal stripes)

MAKE IT

1. Create 1 pink/white diamond-in-a-square unit (see page 152).

2. Create 4 green/white QST units (see page 156).

3. Create 4 navy/pink/white diagonal stripe units (see page 151).

4. Assemble the block by stitching 3 rows of 3 units each. Press.

SPIN THE BOTTLE

Grid: 3x3

(4) burst units in gold

(4) fancy QST units in teal & orange

(1) diamond-in-a-square unit in teal

CUTTING

WHITE FABRIC
(1) 4½" square (diamond)
(8) 5½" x 2½" rectangles (bursts)
(4) 4½" x 2½" rectangles (fancy QSTs)

TEAL FABRIC
(4) 2½" squares (diamond)
(2) 4⅞" squares (fancy QSTs)
(4) 4½" x 2½" rectangles (fancy QSTs)

ORANGE FABRIC
(2) 4⅞" squares (fancy QSTs)

GOLD FABRIC
(4) 4¾" squares (bursts)

MAKE IT

1. Create 4 fancy teal/orange/white QST units (see page 152).

2. Make 4 photocopies of Template A at 100% (see page 169) and foundation piece 4 gold/white units (see page 158).

3. Create 1 teal/white diamond-in-a-square unit (see page 152).

4. Assemble the block by stitching 3 rows of 3 units each. Press.

10 | HAPPY DAYS

Grid: 3x3

(4) plain rectangles in coral

(1) diamond-in-a-square unit in plum

(4) flying geese units in plum

CUTTING

WHITE FABRIC
(1) 4½" square (diamond-in-a-square)
(4) 4½" x 2½" rectangles (geese)
(4) 4½" squares (curves)
  subcut into 4 of Template Q1

PLUM FABRIC
(12) 2½" squares (diamond-in-a-square & geese)

CORAL FABRIC
(4) 4½" x 2½" rectangles (plain units)

GREEN FABRIC
(4) 4½" squares (curves)
  subcut into 4 of Template Q2

(4) curved units in green

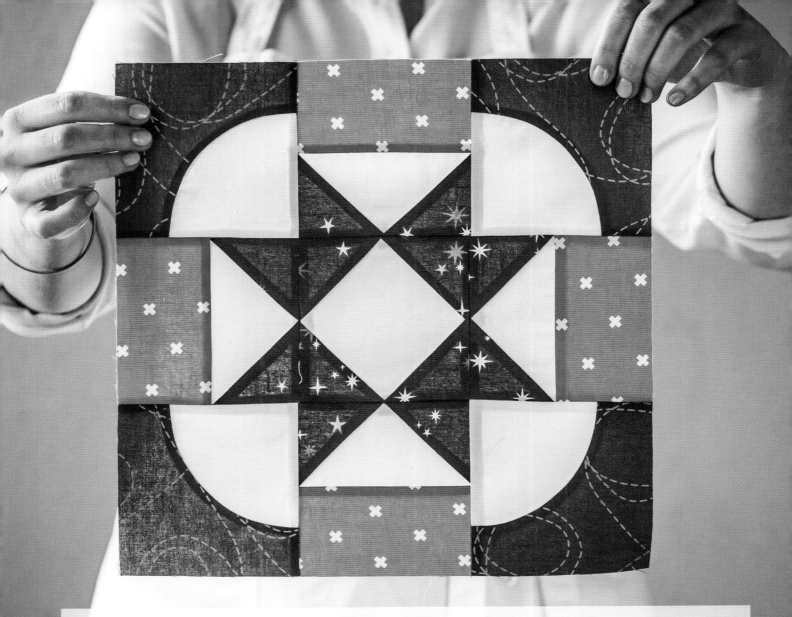

MAKE IT

1. Create 4 green/white curved units (see page 151) using the Templates on page 173.

2. Create 1 plum/white diamond-in-a-square unit (see page 152).

3. Create 4 plum/white flying geese units (see page 153) using the remaining 8 plum squares. Stitch each flying geese unit to a coral rectangle so the white point of the flying geese unit is facing away from the coral rectangle. Press.

4. Assemble the block by stitching 3 rows of 3 units each. Press.

DREAM WEAVER

Grid: 3x3

(5) stripe units in blue →

← *(4) stripe units in yellow*

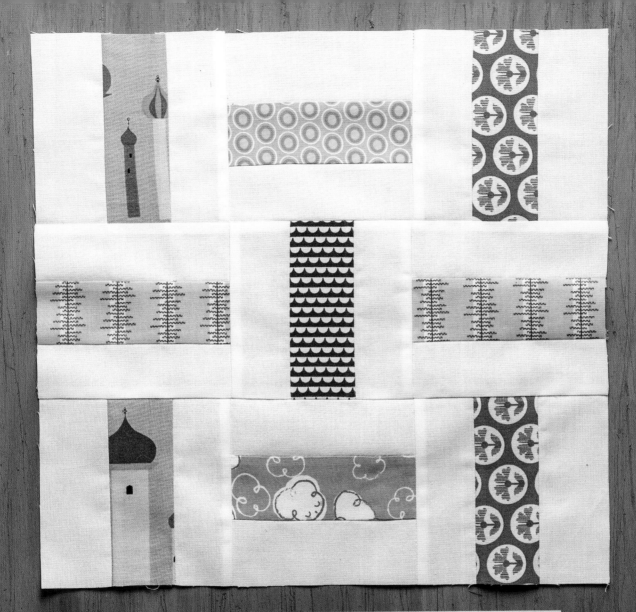

CUTTING

WHITE FABRIC
(18) 4½" x 1⅞" rectangles

BLUE FABRIC
(5) 4½" x 1⅞" rectangles

YELLOW FABRIC
(4) 4½" x 1⅞" rectangles

MAKE IT

1. Create 5 blue/white and 4 yellow/white pieced stripe units (see page 157). Trim units to 4½" square, centering the middle stripe.

2. Assemble the block by stitching 3 rows of 3 units each. Press.

(1) plain square in plum

(4) petal units in gray

(4) HSR units in plum

CUTTING

WHITE FABRIC
(4) 4½" x 2½" rectangles
(4) 4½" squares (petal units)

PLUM FABRIC
(1) 4½" square (center)
(4) 4½" x 2½" rectangles

GRAY FABRIC
(4) Template D4 (petal)
Double-sided fusible webbing is bonded to the wrong side of this fabric before the petals are cut.

MAKE IT

1. Photocopy the Template D4 (see page 172), then trace, cut and appliqué (see page 161) 4 gray fabric petals to the white squares, centered.

2. Create 4 plum/white HSR units (see page 154). Press.

3. Assemble the block by stitching 3 rows of 3 units each. Press.

Grid: 3x3

CUTTING

WHITE FABRIC
(4) 1⅞" squares (snowball)
(8) 4½" x 1⅞" rectangles
(stripes)
(2) 5¼" squares (half-QSTs)

PINK FABRIC
(1) 4½" square (snowball)

ORANGE FABRIC
(4) 4½" x 1⅞" rectangles
(stripes)

DARK TEAL FABRIC
(4) 4⅞" squares (half-QSTs)

LIGHT TEAL FABRIC
(2) 5¼" squares (half-QSTs)

(4) striped units in orange

(4) half-QST units in dark and light teal

(1) snowball unit in pink

MAKE IT

1. Create 1 pink/white snowball unit (see page 157).

2. Create 4 orange/white pieced stripe units (see page 157). Press seams away from the white fabric. Trim units to 4½" square, centering the middle stripe.

3. Create 4 half-QST units (see page 154) Using 2 white squares and 6 teal squares will yield a total of 8 half-QST units. Choose only 4 like-units for this block.

4. Assemble the block by stitching 3 rows of 3 units each. Press.

CHEERIO DARLING

Grid: 3x3

(1) snowball unit in pink and navy

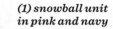

(4) HSR units in navy and gray

(4) diagonal stripe units in gray and navy

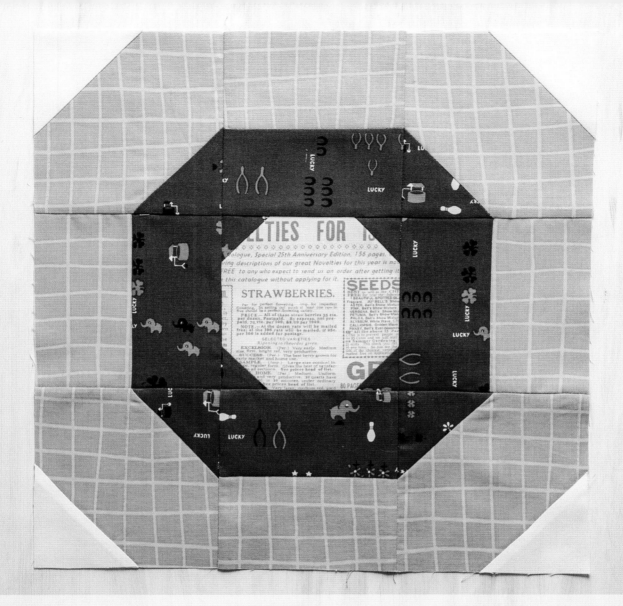

CUTTING

PINK FABRIC
(1) 4½" square (snowball)

NAVY FABRIC
(4) 1½" squares (snowball)
(4) 4½" x 2½" rectangles (HSRs)
(4) 2½" squares (diagonal stripes)

GRAY FABRIC
(4) 4½" x 2½" rectangles (HSRs)
(4) 4½" squares (diagonal stripes)

WHITE FABRIC
(4) 2½" squares (diagonal stripes)

MAKE IT

1. Create a pink/navy snowball unit (see page 157).

2. Create 4 navy/gray HSR units (see page 154).

3. Create 4 navy/gray/white diagonal stripe units (see page 151).

4. Assemble the block by stitching 3 rows of 3 units each. Press.

KINGS CROSS

Grid: 3x3

(1) plain square in white

(4) diamond-in-a-square units in green

(4) fancy HST units in red and navy

CUTTING

WHITE FABRIC
(1) 4½" square (center)
(16) 2½" squares (diamond-in-a-square)
(4) 2⅞" squares
  Cut in half diagonally (fancy HST)

GREEN FABRIC
(4) 4½" squares (diamond-in-a-square)

NAVY FABRIC
(4) 2½" squares (fancy HST)

RED FABRIC
(2) 4⅞" squares
  Cut in half diagonally (fancy HST)

MAKE IT

1. Create 4 green/white diamond-in-a-square units (see page 152).

2. Construct 4 navy/red/white fancy HST units (see page 152). Press seams toward the red.

3. Assemble the block by stitching 3 rows of 3 units each. Press.

RECIPE 16 | MANGO TANGO

Grid: 3x3

CUTTING

WHITE FABRIC
(2) 5" squares (HST)
(4) 5¼" squares (half-QST)

YELLOW FABRIC
(3) 5" squares (HST)
(1) 5¼" square (half-QST)

GREEN FABRIC
(3) 5" squares (HST)
(1) 5¼" square (half-QST)

(2) HST units in yellow

(2) HST units in green

(1) half-QST unit in yellow
(1) half-QST unit in green

(2) half-QST units in yellow and green, and with alternating patch placements

(1) HST unit in yellow and green

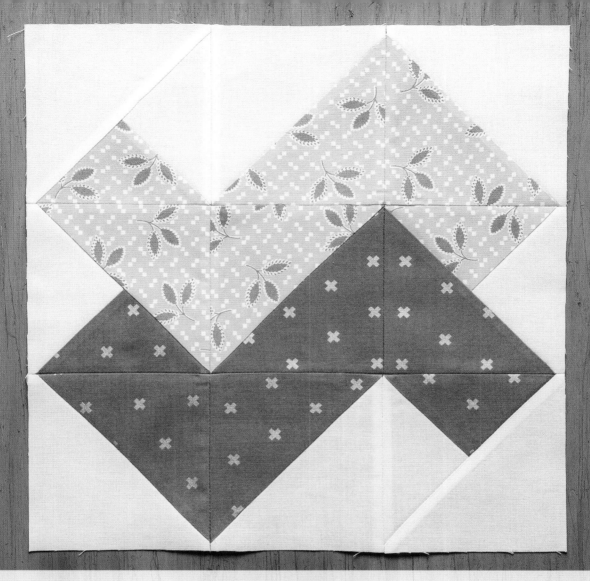

MAKE IT

1. Create 2 white/yellow, 2 white/green, and 2 yellow/green units from 5" squares for a total of 6 HST units (see page 155). Discard 1 yellow/green unit.

2. Create 2 white/yellow and 2 white/green HST units, using the 5¼" squares.

3. Create a half-QST unit (see page 154) using a yellow/white HST from Step 2 with a 5" green square, to create a pair of half-QST units. Identify which matches the unit at the middle right row. Discard the other.

4. Repeat Step 3, to create 3 more pairs of half-QST units (1 green/white HST with a white square, 1 green/white HST with a yellow square, and 1 yellow/white HST with a white square). Of these 6 units, identify the 3 blocks to add to the bottom right, middle left and top left of the block. Discard the other 3.

5. Press all 9 units, and trim each to 4½" square.

6. Assemble the block by stitching 3 rows of 3 units each. Press.

CAMPFIRE

Grid: 3x3

(4) flying geese units with white centers

(1) diamond-in-a-square unit in yellow

(4) flying geese units with pink centers

(4) partial diamond-in-a-square units in blue

CUTTING

WHITE FABRIC
(4) 4½" x 2½" rectangles (geese)
(24) 2½" squares (geese and diamond-in-squares)

YELLOW FABRIC
(1) 4½" square (diamond-in-square)

PINK FABRIC
(8) 2½" squares (geese)
(4) 4½" x 2½" rectangles (geese)

BLUE FABRIC
(4) 4½" squares (partial diamond-in-squares)

MAKE IT

1. Create 1 yellow /white unit and 4 blue/white diamond-in-a-square units (see page 152) omitting 1 of the corner squares on the blue units. Press.

2. Create 8 pink/white flying geese units (see page 153) with alternating fabric placement.

3. Referencing the block photograph above, stitch each goose unit to another goose unit of the opposite color placement. Repeat for a total of 4 units.

4. Assemble the block by stitching 3 rows of 3 units each. Press.

(4) plus sign units in varied cool colors

(5) petal units in pink

CUTTING

WHITE FABRIC
(5) 4½" squares (petals)
(16) 1⅞" squares (plus signs)

PINK FABRIC
(5) of Template D4 (petals)
Double-sided fusible web is bonded to the wrong side of this fabric before the petals are cut

FOUR VARIED COOL FABRICS, EACH
(1) 4½" x 1⅞" rectangle
(2) 1⅞" squares

MAKE IT

1. Photocopy Template D4 (see page 172). Trace, cut and appliqué (see page 161) 5 pink fabric petals to each of the white squares, centered.

2. Create 4 varied cool/white plus sign units (see page 156). Trim to 4½" square.

3. Assemble the block by stitching 3 rows of 3 units each. Press.

19 | MOON BUG

Grid: 3x3

(1) 4-petal unit in green and yellow

(4) triangle units in green and stripes

CUTTING

WHITE FABRIC
(4) 1¾" x 4½" rectangles (corner stripes)
(4) 1¾" x 3¼" rectangles (corner stripes)
(4) 1⅞" squares (corner stripes)

YELLOW FABRIC
(4) 1⅞" x 3¼" rectangles (corner stripes)
(4) 1⅞" squares (corner stripes)
(4) Template D1 (petals)
Double-sided fusible web is bonded to the wrong side of this fabric before the petals are cut

GREEN FABRIC
(1) 4½" square (petal center)
(4) 5" squares (triangles)

STRIPED FABRIC
(8) 5½" x 3" rectangles (triangles)

(4) corner stripe units in yellow

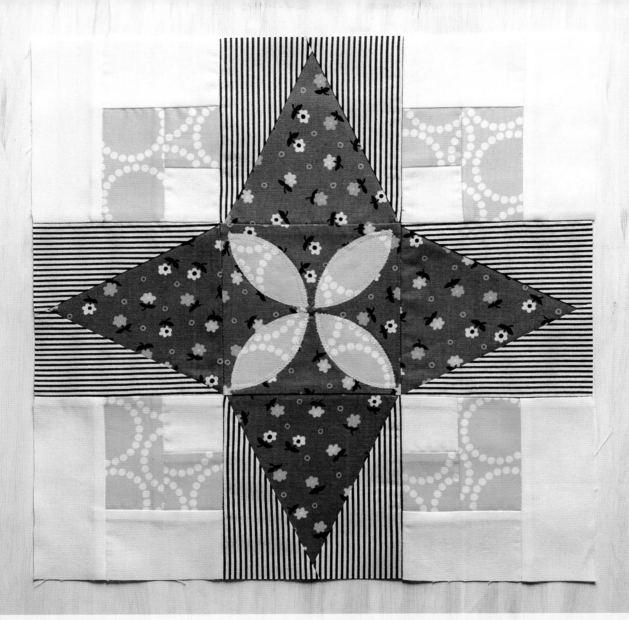

MAKE IT

1. Photocopy Template D1 (see page 172), then trace cut and appliqué (see page 161) 4 yellow fabric petals to the 4½" green square, tips centered.

2. Make 4 copies of Template B at 100% (see page 171). Foundation piece (see page 158) the 4 green/navy triangle units.

3. Using all of the remaining pieces, stitch the corner stripe units (see page 150). After the yellow 1⅞" x 3¼" piece is sewn, trim to 3⅛" square. Trim final unit to 4½" square.

4. Assemble the block by stitching 3 rows of 3 units each. Press.

BON BON

Grid: 3x3

CUTTING

WHITE FABRIC
(12) 2½" squares (geese)
(12) 1½" squares (snowballs)
(3) 4½" x 1½" rectangles
(narrow stripes)
(4) 4½" x 2" rectangles
(wide stripes)

ORANGE FABRIC
(1) 4½" square (snowball)
(2) 4½" x 2½" rectangles
(geese)

BLUE FABRIC
(1) 4½" square (snowball)
(2) 4½" x 2½" rectangles
(geese)

PINK FABRIC
(1) 4½" square (snowball)
(2) 4½" x 2½" rectangles
(geese)

GREEN FABRIC
(3) 4½" x 1½" rectangles
(stripes)

(1) narrow stripe unit in green

(2) wide stripe units in green

(1) snowball unit in orange
(1) snowball unit in blue
(1) snowball unit in pink

(1) narrow rectangle in white

(2) flying geese in orange

(2) flying geese in blue

(2) flying geese in pink

MAKE IT

1. Create 3 snowball units (see page 157) using the orange, blue and pink fabrics.

2. Create 2 orange/white, 2 blue/white and 2 pink/white flying geese units (see page 153) for a total of 6 geese.

3. With the remaining pieces (minus 1 narrow white rectangle) stitch 2 of the wider green/white stripe units (see page 157) and 1 of the narrower green/white stripe unit. Press.

4. Assemble the block by stitching 3 rows of 3 units each, placing the remaining narrow white strip to the left side of the bottom row. Press.

Grid: 4x4

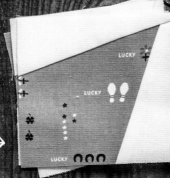

(4) wide bursts in pink

(8) diagonal stripes in teal

(4) wide bursts in green

CUTTING

WHITE FABRIC
(16) 4¼" x 2" (wide bursts)
(16) 2¼" x 2¼" (diagonal stripes)

GREEN FABRIC
(4) 4" squares (wide bursts)

PINK FABRIC
(4) 4" squares (wide bursts)

TEAL FABRIC
(8) 3½" squares (diagonal stripes)

MAKE IT

1. Make 8 photocopies of Template A1 at 75% scale (see page 168). Foundation piece 4 pink/white and 4 green/white units (see page 158).

2. Create 8 diagonal stripe units (see page 151) using the remaining fabrics.

3. Assemble the block by stitching 4 rows of 4 units each. Press.

SUGARPLUM

Grid: 4x4

(8) curved units in pink

(4) plain rectangles in white

(4) plain squares in pink

(1) diamond-in-a-square unit in aqua

(4) bursts in gold

CUTTING

WHITE FABRIC
(1) 3½" square (diamond-in-a-square)
(4) 3½" x 2" rectangles (9-patch)
(8) 4¼" x 2" (bursts)
(8) 3½" squares
   subcut into 8 of Template E3 (curves)

AQUA FABRIC
(4) 2" squares (diamond-in-a-square)

PINK FABRIC
(4) 2" squares (9-patch)
(8) Template F3 (curves)

GOLD FABRIC
(4) 5½" x 2½" (bursts)

MAKE IT

1. Create an aqua/white diamond-in-a-square unit (see page 152).

2. Create a 9-patch using the diamond-in-a-square, white rectangles and pink squares (3 rows of 3 units each).

3. Photocopy both Templates E3 and F3 (see page 173). Create 8 curved units (see page 151) using the white and pink fabrics.

4. Stitch 8 pink/white curved units into 4 pairs. Press.

5. Make 4 photocopies of Template A (see page 169) at 75% scale, then foundation paper piece (see page 158) using the gold and white fabric.

6. Arrange and stitch the assembled units into 3 rows of 3 sections each. Press.

MORNING PAPER

Grid: 4x4

(4) half-QST units in green and text

CUTTING

WHITE FABRIC
(2) 4¼" squares (half-QSTs)
(8) 2" squares (diagonal stripes)

GREEN FABRIC
(2) 4¼" squares (half-QSTs)

TEXT FABRIC
(4) 3⅞" squares (half-QSTs)
(4) 6½" x 3½" rectangles (geese)

DARK TEAL FABRIC
(12) 3½" squares (geese & diagonal stripes)

(4) diagonal stripe units in dark teal

(4) flying geese in dark teal and text

MAKE IT

1. Construct 4 text/green HST units (see page 155). Create 8 text/green/white half-QST units (see page 154). Trim to 3½" square. Of these 8 units, select 4 units with identical fabric placement, with the pinwheel spinning in your preferred direction.

2. Stitch the 4 half-QST units into 2 rows of 2, press, then join the rows, creating the inner pinwheel section. Press.

3. Construct 4 text/dark teal flying geese units (see page 153).

4. Create 4 diagonal stripe units (see page 151) using the remaining dark teal/white fabrics.

5. Arrange the block and stitch into 3 rows of 3 units each. Join rows. Press.

SUN KISSED

Grid: 4x4

(1) snowball unit in yellow and orange

(4) triangle units in orange

CUTTING

WHITE FABRIC
(8) 4" squares (triangles)
(8) 2" squares (4-patches)

YELLOW FABRIC
(1) 6½" (snowball)
(4) 2⅞" x 5¾" rectangles (triangles)

ORANGE FABRIC
(12) 2⅞" x 5¾" rectangles (triangles)
(4) 2" squares (snowball)

BLUE FABRIC
(8) 2" squares (4-patches)

(4) triangle units in orange and yellow

(4) 4-patch units in blue

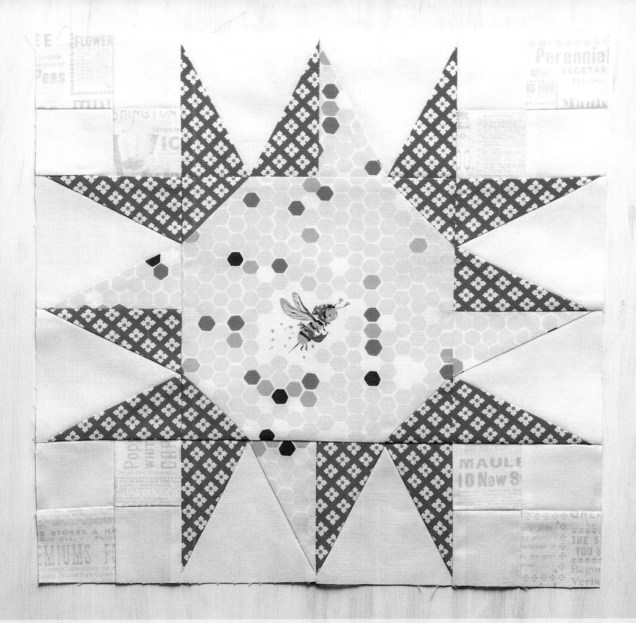

MAKE IT

1. Create 1 yellow/orange snowball unit (see page 157).

2. Make 8 photocopies of Template B at 75% scale (page 171), then foundation paper piece 4 orange/white units and 4 orange/yellow/white units for a total of 8 triangle units (see page 158).

3. Use the remaining squares to stitch (4) 4-patch units, alternating the fabrics and pressing the seams in opposite directions.

4. Referring to the block photograph above, stitch the triangle units into 4 pairs. Press the seams open.

5. Arrange the block and stitch the assembled units into 3 rows of 3 sections each. Join the rows. Press.

MAYBERRY

Grid: 4x4

(8) curved units in medium print

(1) appliqué flower unit in green

(4) petal units in green

CUTTING

WHITE FABRIC
(1) 6½" square (center unit)
(12) 3½" squares (all units)
 subcut 8 squares into Template E3

PRINT FABRIC
8 of Template F3 (curves)

GREEN FABRIC
8 of Template D3 (petals)

Double-sided fusible webbing is bonded to the wrong side of the green fabric before the petals are cut

MAKE IT

1. Photocopy Template D3 (see page 172), then trace, cut and appliqué (see page 161) 4 green fabric petals to a small white square, centered.

Referencing the block photograph above, appliqué the remaining 4 petals to the large white square.

2. Create 8 print/white curved units (see page 173), piece into pairs for a total of 4 pieced units (see page 151). Press seams toward the print.

3. Arrange the block and stitch into 3 rows. Press.

RECIPE
26 | ALL IN

Grid: 4x4

CUTTING

WHITE FABRIC
(8) 1¾" x 3¼" rectangles
(triangles)
(8) 3½" squares (cut corners)
(2) 4" squares (HSTs)

BLUE FABRIC
(1) 2½" square (star center)
(4) 3" squares (triangles)

RED FABRIC
(12) 2½" squares (plain
squares and cut corners)

PURPLE FABRIC
(2) 4" squares (HSTs)

(1) plain square in blue

(4) plain squares in red

(4) triangle units in blue

(8) cut corner units in red

(4) HST units in purple

MAKE IT

1. Make 4 photocopies of Template B at 50% scale (see page 171). Foundation piece 4 blue/white triangle units (see page 158).

2. Construct the 9-patch (see page 155) for the center star using the 4 triangle units, the blue square, and 4 red squares.

3. Construct 8 red/white cut corner units (see page 150). Arrange into mirror image pairs, so that the red corners are pointing away from the center. Stitch into pairs to create a total of 4 pieced units.

4. Referencing the photograph above, stitch 2 pieced units from Step 3 to two sides of the 9-patch.

5. Construct 4 purple/white HST units (see page 155). Trim units to 3½" square.

6. Arrange and stitch the blocks into 3 rows. Join the rows and press.

RECIPE 27 | HAYRIDE

Grid: 4x4

(4) diagonal stripe units in orange

(4) flying geese units in navy

(1) 9-patch unit in orange

CUTTING

WHITE FABRIC
(12) 2½" squares (9-patch & diagonal stripes)
(8) 3½" squares (geese)

ORANGE FABRIC
(5) 2½" squares (9-patch)
(4) 3½" squares (diagonal stripes)

NAVY FABRIC
(4) 6½" x 3½" rectangles (geese)

MAKE IT

1. Construct 1 orange/white 9-patch unit (see page 155), pressing seams toward the orange.

2. Construct the 4 orange/white diagonal stripe units (see page 151).

3. Construct the 4 navy/white flying geese units (see page 153).

4. Stitch 2 pieced units from Step 3 to two sides of the 9-patch.

5. Arrange and stitch the blocks into 3 rows. Join the rows and press.

SECOND STAR

Grid: 4x4

CUTTING

WHITE FABRIC
(8) 3½" x 2" rectangles
(diamonds)
(4) 6½" x 3½" rectangles
(geese)
(8) 4½" x 2" rectangles
(bursts)

GREEN FABRIC
(8) 3½" x 2" rectangles
(diamonds)
(8) 3½" squares (geese)

YELLOW FABRIC
(8) 3¼" x 2" rectangles
(diamonds)
(4) 5½" x 2½" rectangles
(bursts)

(4) diagonal diamond units in green and yellow

(4) burst units in yellow

(4) flying geese units in green

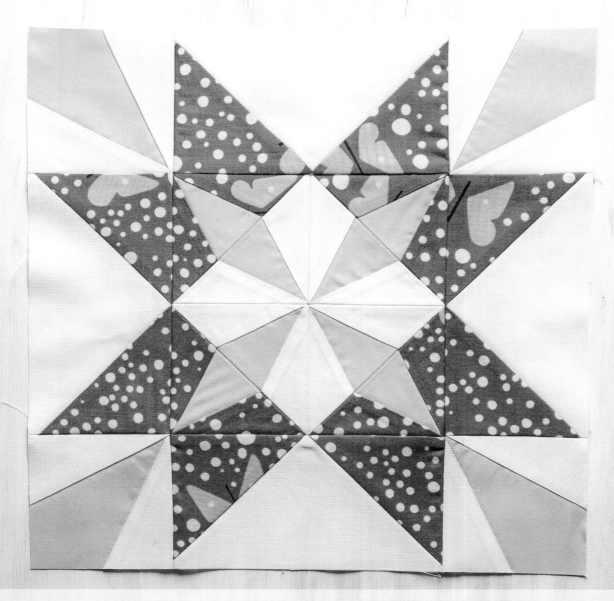

MAKE IT

1. Make 8 photocopies of Template C at 75% scale (see page 170). Foundation Piece 4 yellow/green diamond units (see page 158) and 4 yellow/white units. Referencing the photograph, stitch the diamond units into pairs along the long side to create 4 diagonal diamond units (see page 151). Press seams open.

2. Make 4 photocopies of Template A at 75% scale (see page 169). Foundation piece 4 yellow/white burst units (see page 158).

3. Construct 4 green/white flying geese units (see page 153).

4. Stitch 2 pieced units from Step 3 to two sides of the 9-patch.

5. Arrange and stitch into 3 rows. Join the rows and press.

29 | UNWIND

Grid: 4x4

(2) plain rectangles in navy →

(4) HST units in navy →

(2) plain rectangles in white →

(1) striped unit in 3 greens →

CUTTING

WHITE FABRIC
(2) 6½" x 3½" rectangles (sides)
(2) 4" squares (HSTs)

NAVY FABRIC
(2) 6½" x 3½" rectangles (spool top & bottom)
(2) 4" squares (HSTs)

GREEN FABRICS
(3) 6½" x 2½" rectangles from a variety of green prints (stripe)

MAKE IT

1. Create 4 HST navy/white units (see page 155). Trim units to 3½" square.

2. Stitch the 3 green rectangles together to form a stripe unit (see page 157). Press. Attach a white rectangle to the two sides of the stripe unit.

3. Stitch the block into 3 rows. Join the rows and press.

POP WEED

Grid: 4x4

(1) four petal unit in yellow

(4) flying geese units in red

(4) HSTs in blue

CUTTING

WHITE FABRIC
(1) 6½" square (petal unit)
(4) 6½" x 3½" rectangles (geese)
(2) 4" squares (HSTs)

RED FABRIC
(8) 3½" squares (geese)

BLUE FABRIC
(2) 4" squares (HSTs)

YELLOW FABRIC
(4) of Template D3 (petals)
*Double-sided fusible webbing is
bonded to the wrong side of this
fabric before the petals are cut*

MAKE IT

1. Photocopy Template D3 (see
page 172). Using the photograph
above as a reference for placement,
trace, cut and appliqué (see page
161) the 8 yellow fabric petals to the
white square, centered.

2. Create 4 red/white flying geese
units (see page 153).

3. Create 4 HST units (see page 155)
using the remaining fabrics. Trim the
units to 3½".

4. Stitch the assembled units into
3 rows. Join the rows and press.

31 | PUMPKIN PIE

Grid: 5x5

(4) triangle units in pink

(1) 9-patch unit in brown and navy

VIRGINIA
REBECCA
BLANCHE
SANDRA

(4) plain squares in white

(8) HST units in brown

(1) plain square in navy

CUTTING

WHITE FABRIC
(8) 2⅞" squares (9-patch & corners)
(4) 3⅛" squares (HSTs)
(8) 3½" x 2" rectangles (triangles)

NAVY FABRIC
(1) 2⅞" square (9-patch)

BROWN FABRIC
(4) 2⅞" squares (9-patch)
(4) 3½" squares (HSTs)

PINK FABRIC
(4) 3¼" squares (triangles)

MAKE IT

* Use a scant ¼" seam allowance

1. Construct a navy/brown/white 9-patch unit (see page 155).

2. Make 4 photocopies of Template B at 60% scale (see page 171). Foundation piece 4 pink/white triangle units (see page 158).

3. Construct 8 HST brown/white units (see page 155).

4. Stitch an HST unit to each side of the triangle units, so that the points of the HSTs are facing away from the center. Create a total of 4 pieced units.

5. Referencing the photograph above, attach 2 pieced units from Step 4 to two sides of the 9-patch.

6. Attach a white square to each side of the remaining pieced units. Press seams toward the white squares.

7. Join the 3 rows and press.

FLAG DAY

Grid: 5x5

(4) plain squares in navy →

(4) diagonal stripe units in orange ↓

(1) plain square in white ↖

(4) plain squares in medium neutral ↗

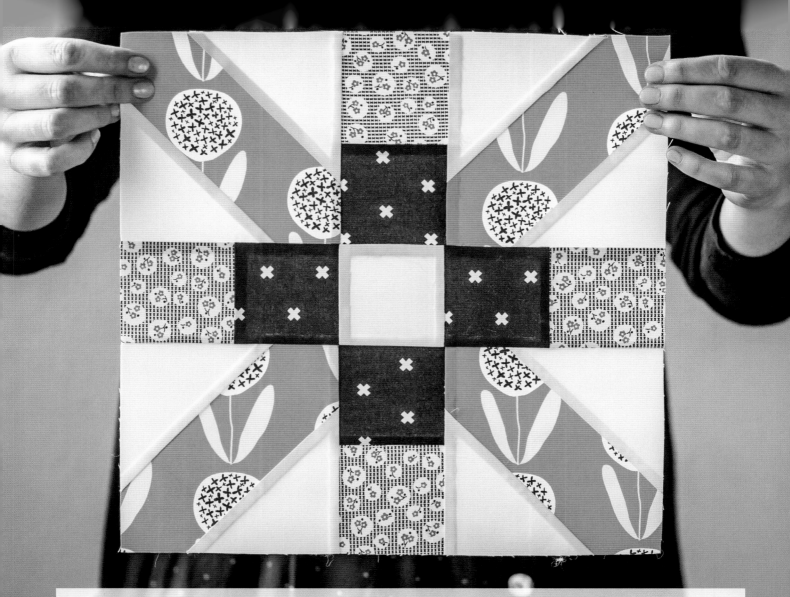

CUTTING

WHITE FABRIC
(1) 2⅞" square (center)
(8) 3¾" squares (diagonal stripe)

ORANGE FABRIC
(4) 5½" squares (diagonal stripe)

NAVY FABRIC
(4) 2⅞" squares (plain)

MEDIUM NEUTRAL FABRIC
(4) 2⅞" squares (plain)

MAKE IT

* Use a scant ¼" seam allowance

1. Construct 4 orange/white diagonal stripe units (see page 151).

2. Stitch each navy square to a medium neutral square, and press toward the navy.

3. Stitch the units into 3 rows, pressing away from the navy. Join the rows and press.

33 | THAT A-WAY

Grid: 5x5

(4) triangle units in red

(4) stripe units in red

(12) HST units in aqua

(1) plain square in red

(4) curved units in blue

CUTTING

WHITE FABRIC
(8) 2⅞" x 1¼" rectangles (stripes)
(8) 3½" x 2" rectangles (triangles)
(4) 2⅞" squares (curves)
(6) 3½" squares (HSTs)

RED FABRIC
(1) 2⅞" square (center)
(4) 2⅞" x 1¼" rectangles (stripes)
(4) 3¼" squares (triangles)

BLUE FABRIC
(4) 3" squares (curves)

AQUA FABRIC
(6) 3½" squares (HSTs)

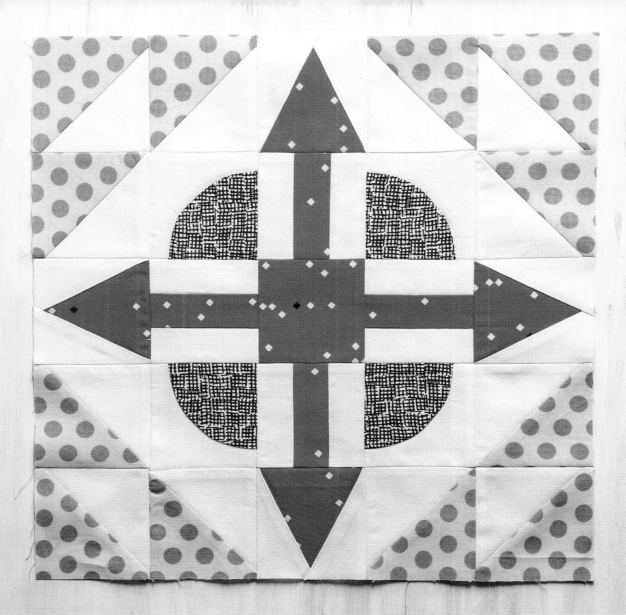

MAKE IT

* Use a scant ¼" seam allowance

1. Construct 4 white/red/white stripe units (see page 157).

2. Subcut 4 navy Template F2 units and 4 white Template E2 units (see page 173). Stitch 4 blue/white curved units (see page 151).

3. Make 4 photocopies of Template B at 60% scale (see page 171). Foundation piece (see page 158) 4 red/white triangle units.

4. Construct 12 aqua/white HST units (see page 155). Trim the units to 2⅞" square.

5. Referring to the block photograph above for placement, arrange and stitch 5 rows of 5 units each. Press. Join rows and press.

RECIPE
34 WOODED

Grid: 5x5

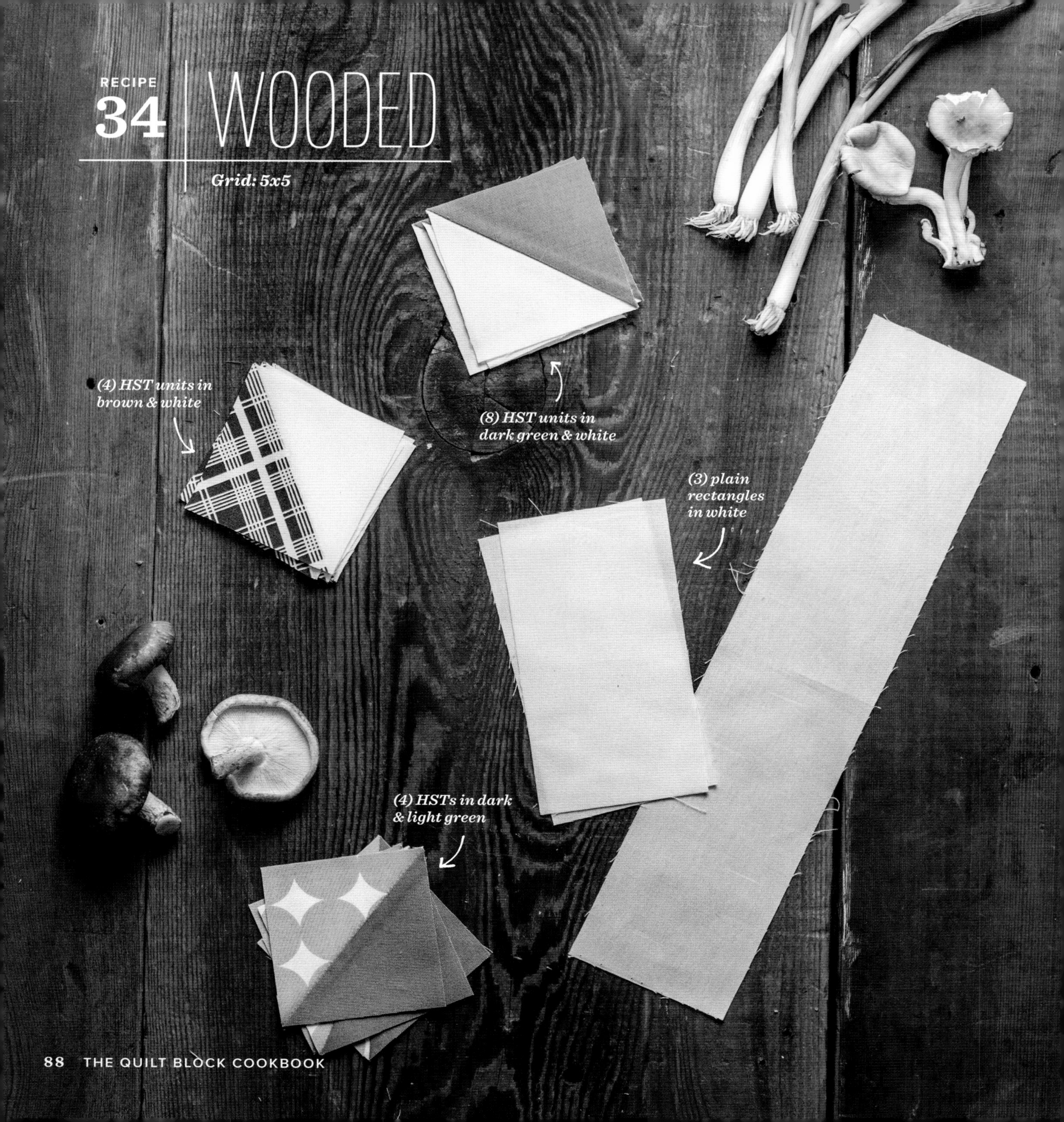
(4) HST units in brown & white
(8) HST units in dark green & white
(3) plain rectangles in white
(4) HSTs in dark & light green

CUTTING

WHITE FABRIC
(1) 12½" x 3" rectangle (horizontal strip)
(2) 5¼" x 3" rectangles (vertical strips)
(6) 3½" squares (HSTs)

DARK GREEN FABRIC
(4) 3½" squares (HSTs)

LIGHT GREEN FABRIC
(2) 3½" squares (HSTs)

BROWN FABRIC
(2) 3½" squares (HSTs)

MAKE IT

* Use a scant ¼" seam allowance

1. Construct 16 HST units (see page 155), 8 white/green, 4 white/brown, 4 light green/dark green. Trim the units to 2⅞" square.

2. Assemble 2 dark green/white units, 1 dark green/light green unit, and 1 brown/white unit into a 4-patch for (4) 4-patch tree units.

3. Attach a short white rectangle between the (2) 4-patch units. Repeat to create 2 vertical units.

4. Attach the vertical units from Step 3 to each side of the remaining white strip. Press.

Grid: 5x5

(4) QST units in purple and aqua

(5) plain squares in white

(8) plain squares in purple

(4) HST units in aqua

(4) QST units in red

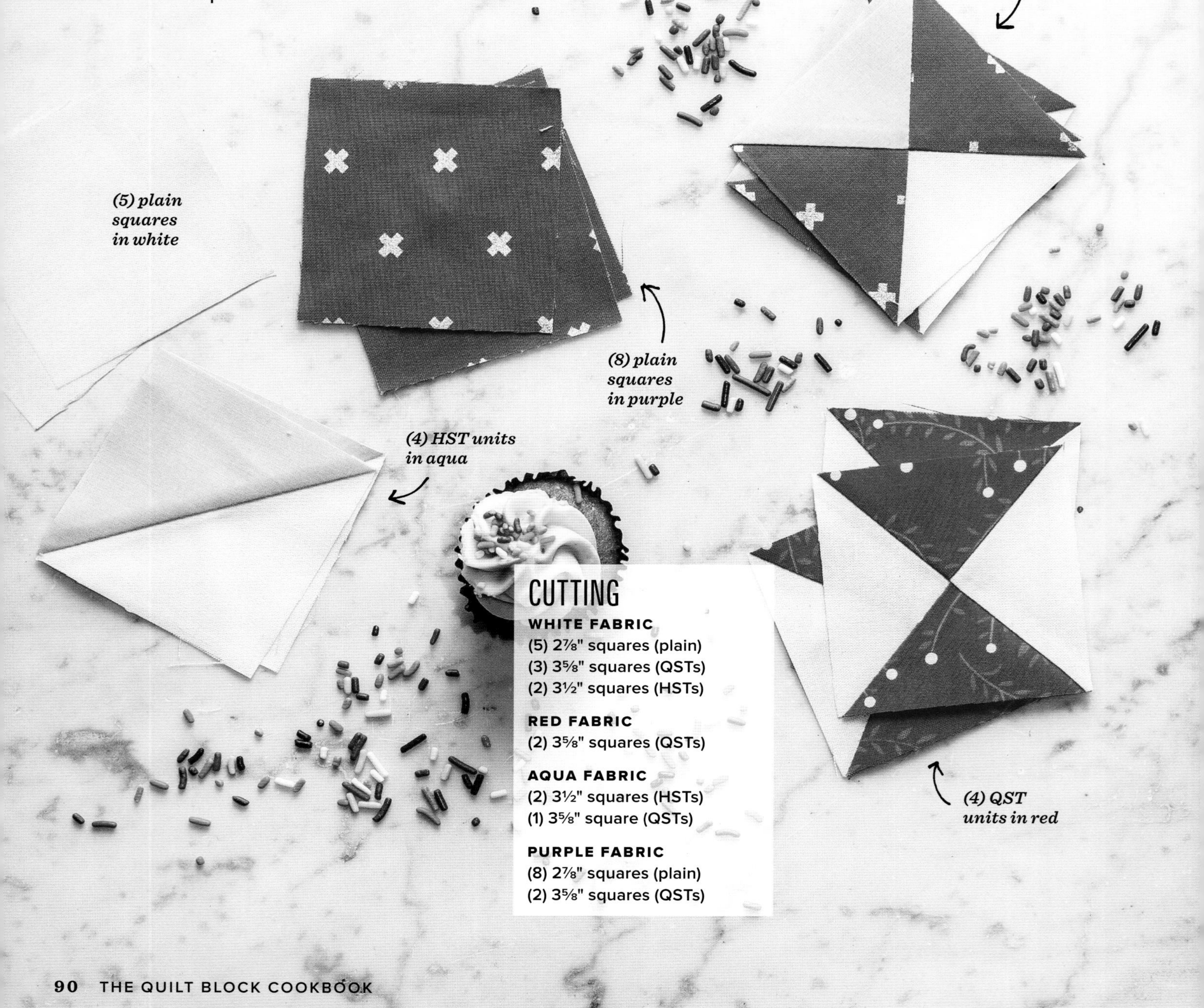

CUTTING

WHITE FABRIC
(5) 2⅞" squares (plain)
(3) 3⅝" squares (QSTs)
(2) 3½" squares (HSTs)

RED FABRIC
(2) 3⅝" squares (QSTs)

AQUA FABRIC
(2) 3½" squares (HSTs)
(1) 3⅝" square (QSTs)

PURPLE FABRIC
(8) 2⅞" squares (plain)
(2) 3⅝" squares (QSTs)

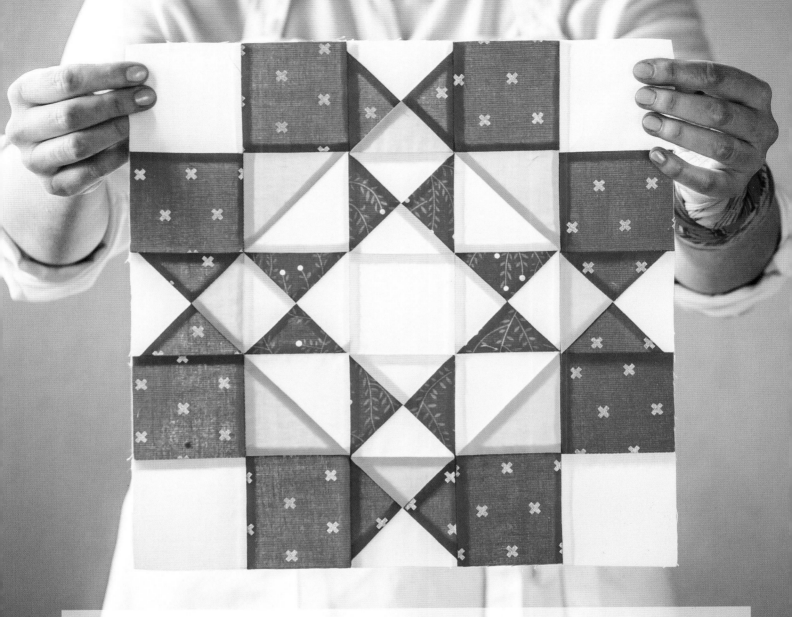

MAKE IT

* Use a scant ¼" seam allowance

1. Construct 4 red/white, 2 purple/white, and 2 purple/aqua for a total of 8 HST units (see page 155). Press but do not trim.

2. Pair the units from Step 1 to create 4 red/white and 4 purple/aqua/white, QST units (see page 156).

3. Construct 4 aqua/white HST units (see page 155).

4. Trim all 12 of the HST and QST units to 2⅞".

5. Again, referencing the above block photograph for placement, arrange and stitch into 5 rows of 5 units each. Join the rows and press.

WINDSONG

Grid: 5x5

(1) plain square in navy

(4) flying geese in dark blue & teal

(4) diagonal diamond units in gray

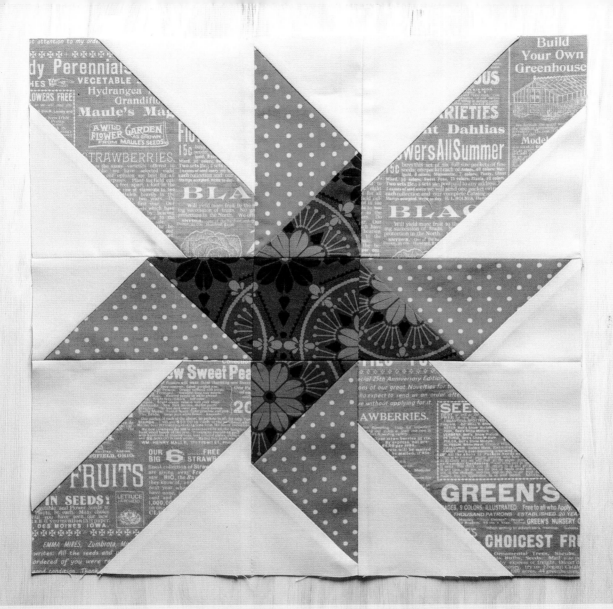

CUTTING

WHITE FABRIC
(8) 3¾" squares (diagonal stripes)
(4) 2⅞" squares (flying geese)

GRAY FABRIC
(4) 5½" squares (diagonal stripes)

DARK BLUE FABRIC
(4) 2⅞" squares (center & geese)

TEAL FABRIC
(4) 2⅞" squares (flying geese)

MAKE IT

* Use a scant ¼" seam allowance

1. Construct 4 gray/white diagonal stripe units (see page 151).

2. Construct 4 teal/dark blue/white flying geese units (see page 153). The white square is added to the left, and the dark blue is added to the right.

3. Arrange and stitch the units into 3 rows of 3 units each. Join the rows. Press.

37 | ICEBOX

Grid: 6x6

(4) plain squares in white

(1) diamond-in-a-square in green

(4) plain squares in red

CUTTING

WHITE FABRIC
(16) 2½" squares (plain, geese, diamond-in-a-square)
(4) 2⅞" squares (half-QSTs)
(4) 4½" x 2½" rectangles (geese)

RED FABRIC
(12) 2½" squares (plain & geese)
(2) 3¼" squares (half-QSTs)
(4) 4½" x 2½" rectangles (geese)

BLUE FABRIC
(2) 3¼" squares (half-QSTs)

GREEN FABRIC
(1) 4½" square (diamond-in-a-square)

(4) flying geese in white with red sides

(8) half-QSTs in red, blue & white

(4) flying geese in red with white sides

MAKE IT

1. Construct 1 green/white diamond-in-a-square unit (see page 152).

2. Referring to the block photograph for placement, construct 4 red/white and 4 white/red flying geese (see page 153) for a total of 8 units.

3. Construct 4 red/blue HST units (see page 155). Press these units but do not trim.

4. Pair the HST units from Step 3 with a 2⅞" square, and create 8 half-QST units (see page 154). In half of the units, the placement of the red/blue triangles will be reversed. Press and trim these units to 2½".

5. Arrange and stitch into 5 rows of 5 units each. Join the rows and press.

Grid: 6x6

(2) flying geese units in yellow

(4) HST units in yellow

(8) HST units in pink

(4) plain square units in white

(2) flying geese units in pink

(2) flying geese units in green

(1) QST unit in pink

(2) flying geese units in white with yellow sides

CUTTING

WHITE FABRIC
(1) 5¼" square (QST)
(12) 2½" squares (flying geese and plain)
(6) 3" squares (HSTs)
(4) 4½" x 2½" rectangles (flying geese)

PINK FABRIC
(1) 5¼" square (QST)
(4) 3" squares (HSTs)
(4) 2½" squares (flying geese)

YELLOW FABRIC
(2) 4½" x 2½" rectangles (flying geese)
(2) 3" squares (HSTs)
(4) 2½" squares (flying geese)

GREEN FABRIC
(2) 4½" x 2½" rectangles (flying geese)

MAKE IT

1. Construct 1 pink/white QST (see page 156).

2. Set aside (4) 2½" white squares for the corners. Use the remaining 2½" squares and 4½" x 2½" rectangles to piece the 8 varied flying geese units (see page 153) 2 green/white, 2 pink/white, 2 yellow/white, 2 white/yellow.

3. Construct 8 pink/white and 4 yellow/white for a total of 12 HST units (see page 155).

4. Arrange and stitch into 5 rows. Join the rows. Press.

RECIPE

39 CRISS CROSS APPLESAUCE

Grid: 6x6

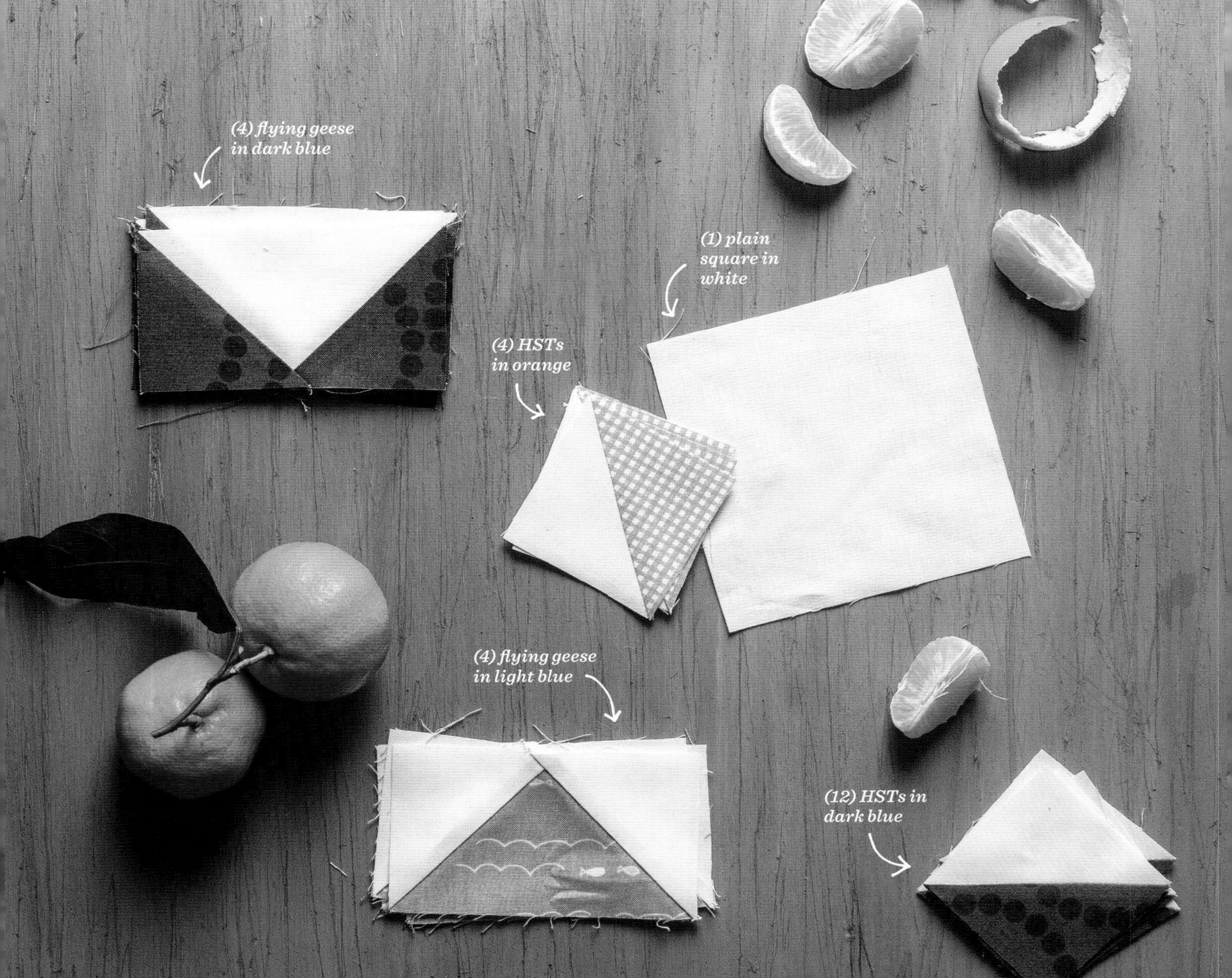
(4) flying geese in dark blue
(1) plain square in white
(4) HSTs in orange
(4) flying geese in light blue
(12) HSTs in dark blue

CUTTING

WHITE FABRIC
(1) 4½" square (plain)
(8) 3" squares (HSTs)
(8) 2½" squares (flying geese)
(4) 4½" x 2½" rectangles (flying geese)

DARK BLUE FABRIC
(6) 3" squares (HSTs)
(8) 2½" squares (flying geese)

LIGHT BLUE FABRIC
(4) 4½" x 2½" rectangles (flying geese)

ORANGE FABRIC
(2) 3" squares (HSTs)

MAKE IT

1. Construct 4 light blue/white and 4 dark blue/white for a total of 8 flying geese units (see page 153).

2. Construct 12 dark blue/white and 4 orange/white for a total of 16 HST units (see page 155). Press and trim to 2½".

3. Referencing the photograph above, arrange and stitch into 5 rows of 5 units each. Join the rows and press.

(1) plain square in white

(4) HST units in aqua

(8) plain squares in white

(4) HST units in dark pink

(4) flying geese units in light floral

(4) flying geese units in dark pink

May 16
Accept our thanks, Heavenly Father, for these and all other blessings for Jesus' sake. Amen.

May 17
Receive, we pray Thee, our gratitude, feed all mankind, we pray Thee, as Thou hast fed us. Deliver us from evil, and the effects of evil. And when Thou art done with us here on earth, own and receive us into Thy kingdom above, we ask in Thy name. Amen.

May 18
Our Father, we thank Thee for this expression of Thy loving kindness to us. Guide us by Thy Spirit into all truth and bring us to Thyself in Heaven, through Jesus Christ our Lord. Amen.

66

May 19
Our Heavenly Father, we pray Thee to acc our thanks for the blessings before us wh are an expression of Thy constant love a care. Sanctify them to us and us to T service, for Jesus' sake. Amen.

May 20
Accept our heartfelt thanks, our Father, for the food Thou hast spread before us and pardon our sins for Christ's sake. Amen.

May 21
Our Heavenly Father, we acknowledge that every good and perfect gift cometh from Thee. Now, unto Thee do we return most hearty thanks for these material gifts. Strengthen us by them, that we may have life to use for the glory of Thy kingdom in doing service for Thee. And unto Thee be all honor. now and forevermore. Amen.

67

CUTTING

WHITE FABRIC
(1) 4½" square (plain)
(28) 2½" squares (flying geese and plain)
(4) 3" squares (HSTs)

LIGHT FLORAL FABRIC
(4) 4½" x 2½" rectangles (flying geese)

DARK PINK FABRIC
(4) 4½" x 2½" rectangles (flying geese)
(2) 3" squares (HSTs)

AQUA FABRIC
(2) 3" squares (HSTs)

MAKE IT

1. Construct 4 floral/white and 4 dark pink /white flying geese for a total of 8 units (see page 153).

2. Construct 4 dark pink/white and 4 aqua/white HSTs for a total of 8 units (see page 155). Trim to 2½".

3. Arrange and stitch into 5 rows of 5 units each. Join the rows. Press.

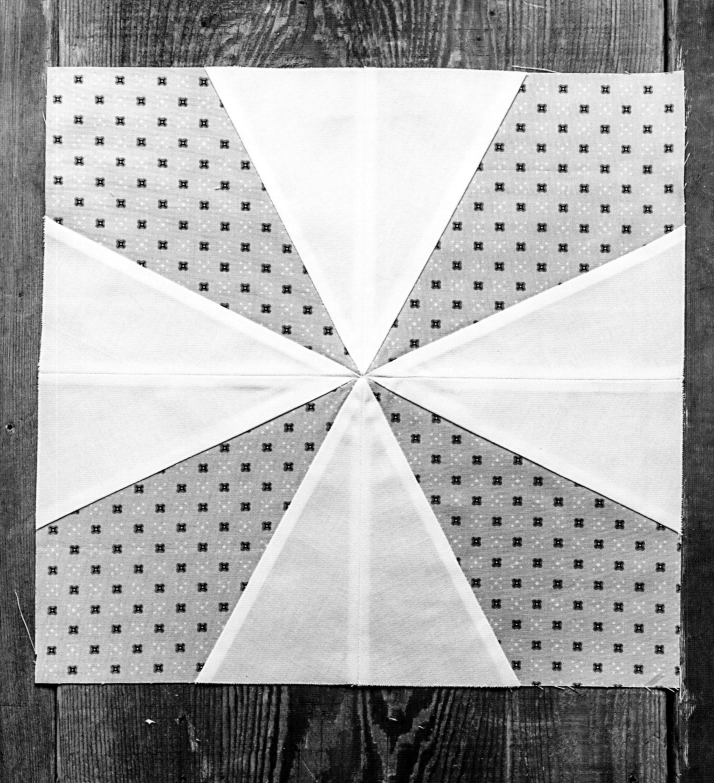

STAPLE BLOCKS

I love the simple tastes in life—fresh strawberries, strong coffee, and melty cheese. That's why I adore staple blocks. They're bold, they're quick, they show off fabrics well, and not only do they look fabulous in a quilt on their own, they also make the perfect pairing for more complex blocks. Alternate your favorite fancy blocks with one of these sweet simples for a dynamic quilt that's anything but ordinary. Browse the Perfect Pairings chapter for inspiration (pg 162).

(4) curved units in orange with white cut corners

CUTTING

ORANGE FABRIC
(4) 6½" squares, each in a different print
subcut each with Template E5

WHITE FABRIC
(4) 6" squares
subcut each with Template F5
(4) 3¼" squares

MAKE IT

1. Photocopy Templates E5 and F5 at 100% (see page 173). Construct 4 orange/white curved units (see page 151).

2. Using the stitch and flip technique (see page 149), attach a 3¼" square opposite the curve on each unit.

3. Stitch the units into 2 rows of 2 units each. Press the seams in opposite directions. Join the rows and press.

RECIPE 42

ALL IS BRIGHT

Staples

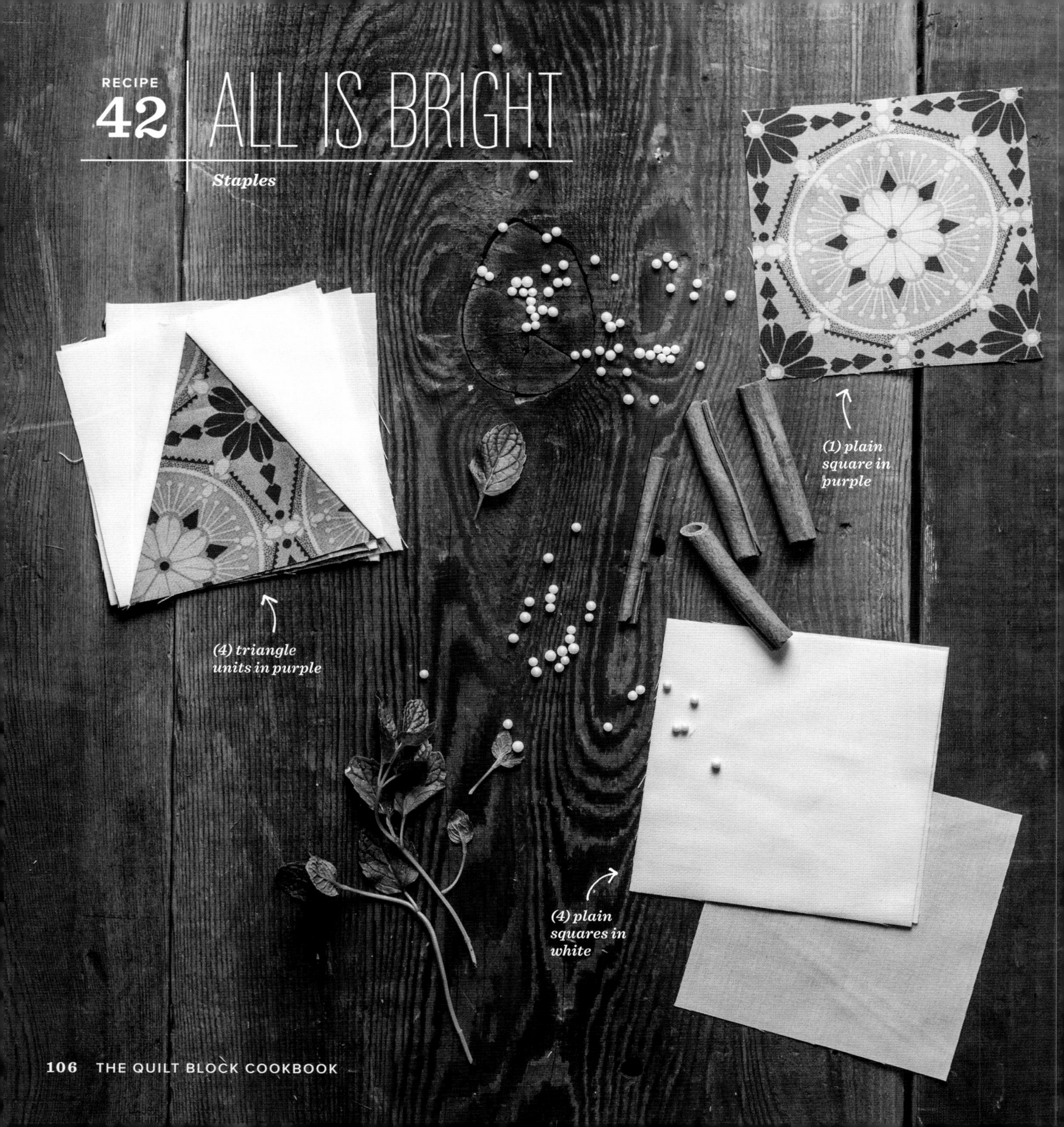
(1) plain square in purple
(4) triangle units in purple
(4) plain squares in white

CUTTING

WHITE FABRIC
(8) 5½" x 3" rectangles (triangles)
(4) 4½" squares (plain)

PURPLE FABRIC
(1) 4½" square (plain)
(4) 5" squares (triangles)

MAKE IT

1. Make 4 photocopies of Template B at 100% (see page 171) and foundation piece 4 purple/white units (see page 158).

2. Assemble 3 rows of 3 units each. Join the rows and press.

43 | ROUND ABOUT

Staples

*(4) HSTs
in green*

*(1) square
in white*

*(4) rectangles
in green stripe*

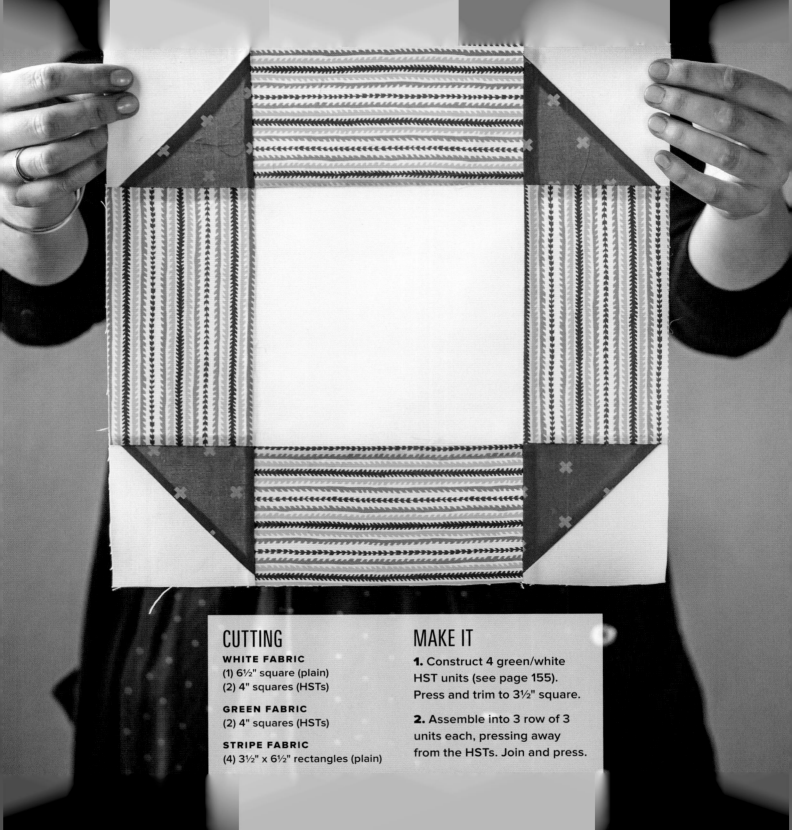

CUTTING

WHITE FABRIC
(1) 6½" square (plain)
(2) 4" squares (HSTs)

GREEN FABRIC
(2) 4" squares (HSTs)

STRIPE FABRIC
(4) 3½" x 6½" rectangles (plain)

MAKE IT

1. Construct 4 green/white HST units (see page 155). Press and trim to 3½" square.

2. Assemble into 3 row of 3 units each, pressing away from the HSTs. Join and press.

PAPER LANTERNS

Staples

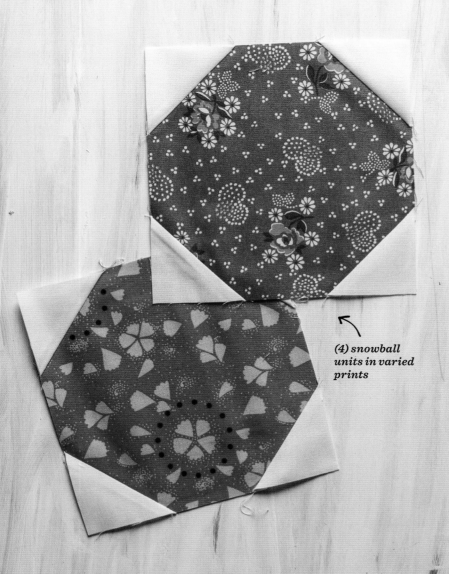

(4) snowball units in varied prints

CUTTING

WHITE FABRIC
(16) 2¼" squares

PRINT FABRICS
(4) 6½" squares

MAKE IT

1. Construct 4 print/white snowball units (see page 157).

2. Arrange and stitch the units into 2 rows of 2 units each, pressing the seams in opposite directions. Join the rows and press.

RECIPE

45 DASH AWAY

Staples

(2) white squares
(1) aqua print
ZEROLL

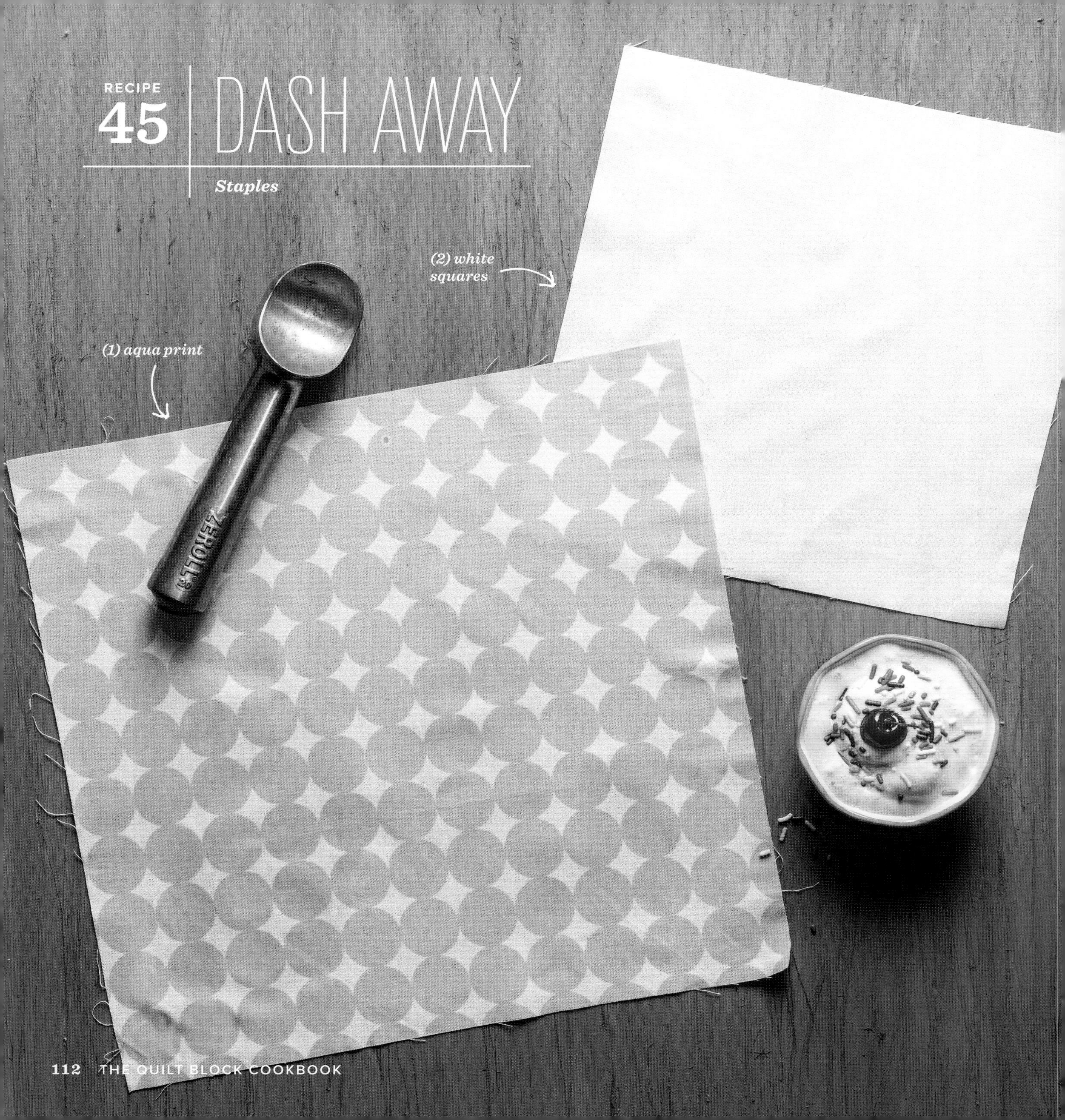

CUTTING

AQUA FABRIC
(1) 12½" square (stripe)

WHITE FABRIC
(2) 9¼" squares (stripe)

MAKE IT

1. Create 1 aqua/white super-sized single diagonal stripe unit (see page 151). Press.

RECIPE
46 | MORE OR LESS

Staples

*(1) plain square
in purple*

*(4) plain
square units
in white*

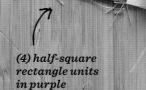

*(4) half-square
rectangle units
in purple*

CUTTING

WHITE FABRIC
(4) 4½" x 2½" rectangles
(4) 4½" squares

PURPLE FABRIC
(1) 4½" square (center)
(4) 4½" x 2½" rectangles

MAKE IT

1. Construct 4 purple/white half-square rectangle units (see page 154).

2. Assemble and stitch into 3 rows of 3 units each. Press.

(2) short plain rectangles in gold

(4) plain squares in white

(1) long plain rectangles in gold

CUTTING

WHITE FABRIC
(4) 5½" squares

GOLD FABRIC
(2) 2½" x 5½" short rectangles
(1) 2½" x 12½" long rectangle

MAKE IT

1. Stitch a white square to each side of the short gold rectangle. Press the seams toward the gold. Repeat.

2. Join rows by stitching the long gold rectangle vertically between the two units from Step 1. Press the seams toward the gold.

(4) plain rectangles in white

(4) plain squares in various purples

(1) 9-patch unit in various purples

CUTTING

WHITE FABRIC
(4) 2⅞" squares
(4) 2⅞" x 7¾" rectangles

VARIOUS PURPLES
(9) 2⅞" squares

MAKE IT

* Use a scant ¼" seam allowance

1. Piece the purple/white 9-patch unit (see page 155). Attach a white rectangle to two sides of the 9-patch. Press toward the 9-patch.

2. Attach a purple square to each side of a white rectangle. Repeat.

3. Arrange and stitch into 3 rows. Join the rows and press.

HOT CROSS BUN

Staples

(4) diagonal stripe units in orange

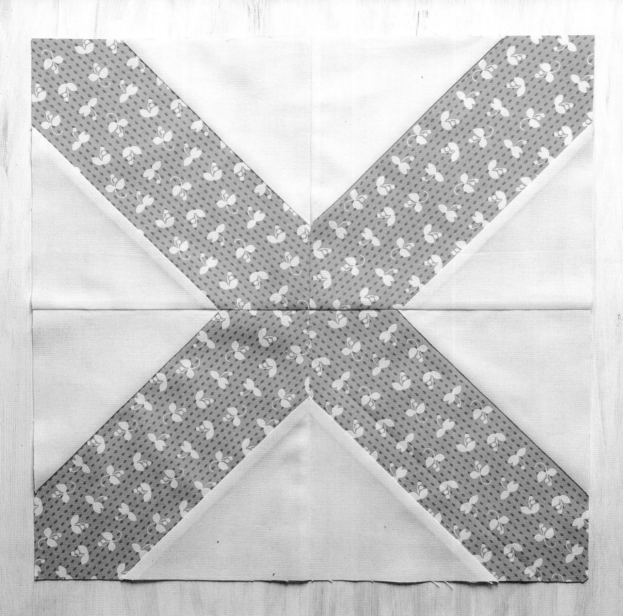

CUTTING

WHITE FABRIC
(8) 4¼" squares

ORANGE FABRIC
(4) 6½" squares

MAKE IT

1. Make 4 orange/white diagonal stripe units (see page 151).

2. Stitch the units into pairs. Join the 2 rows and press.

*(4) burst units
in blue*

CUTTING

WHITE FABRIC
(8) 9" x 5" rectangles

BLUE FABRIC
(4) 7" squares

MAKE IT

1. Print 4 copies of Template A at 150% scale (see page 169). Foundation piece 4 blue/white burst units (see page 158).

2. Arrange and stitch the units into pairs. Join the 2 rows and press.

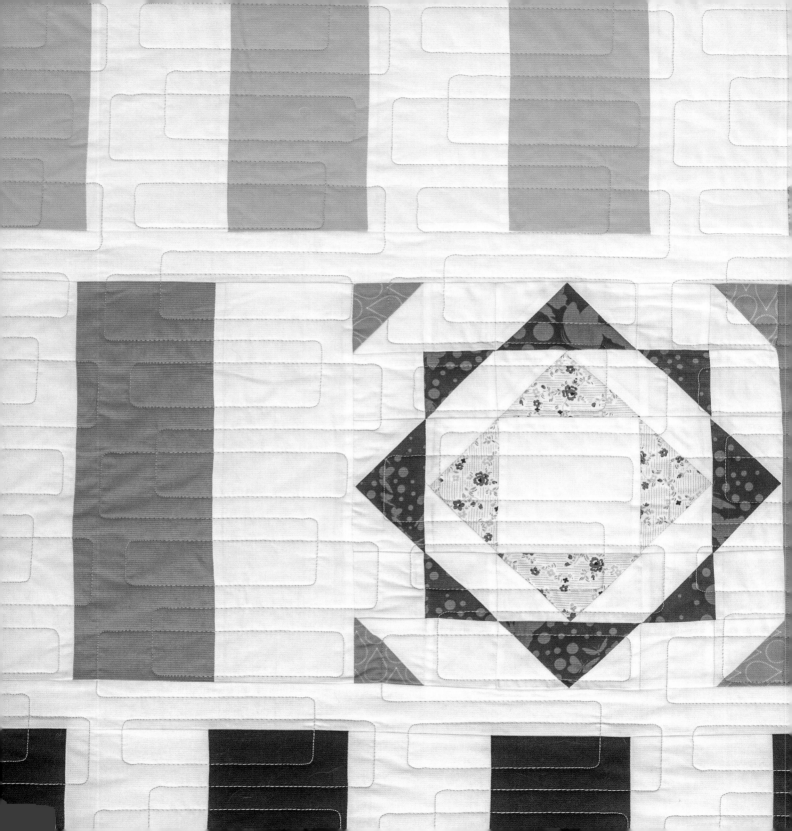

THE
QUILTS

OFF THE GRID

This quilt is an old-school cornerstone sampler that's been given a big city makeover! The bold offset layout and juicy colors will make your blocks happy campers in their new-found home. Choose a background color that contrasts well with your blocks for maximum impact. My light, bright blocks are working together as one—like panes in a fanciful stained glass window. Each block is a part of the bigger picture—bursts of color that seem to float atop a sea of dapper navy, while the striking grid of colorful stripes visually holds everything in place. This yeilds a refreshed version of a classic straight-set.

Quilted by
Amy Wade

Finished Size:
75½" square

INGREDIENTS

FOR THE QUILT TOP
16 of your favorite 12 inch blocks

Navy solid: 5 yards

6 solids of choice for the stripes: ⅛ yard each

Periwinkle solid for the cornerstones: ⅛ yard

FOR THE QUILT BACK
4½ yards

FOR THE BINDING
⅝ yard

CUTTING

NAVY FABRIC
(1) 30½" x 18½" rectangle
(1) 30½" x 5½" rectangle
(1) 17½" x 18½" rectangle
(1) 17½" x 5½" rectangle
(6) 12½" x 5½" rectangles
(6) 12½" x 18½" rectangles
(24) 12½" x 2" rectangles

PERIWINKLE FABRIC
(9) 2" squares

**FROM EACH OF
6 SOLID FABRICS
FOR THE STRIPES**
(1) 2" x 18½" rectangle
(1) 2" x 5½" rectangle

BINDING FABRIC
(8) 2½" x WOF strips

Figure 1

By & Large

Cutting large pieces of fabric can be tricky when the needed sizes are bigger than the rulers or mat you're working with. Make the process more manageable by folding large patches in half, or even quarters to cut. A 30 inch long piece of fabric only needs 15 inches of measuring space when you fold it in half. Also, when measurements exceed those of your rulers, butt two rulers up to one another, or use the markings on your mat. Ruler markings are preferred, when possible, for maximum accuracy.

MAKE IT

1. Arrange the 16 quilt blocks, (24) 12½" x 2" navy pieces (sashing), and (9) 2" periwinkle squares (cornerstones) on your design wall or floor and position the sampler blocks until you are pleased with the composition (Fig. 1). Stitch the 4 rows of blocks and 3 rows of sashing, pressing the seams toward the navy.

2. Join these 7 block and sashing rows, taking care to pin at the seam intersections. Press.

Figure 2

3. Stitch the horizontal stripe sections that go on either side of the inner block section, pressing seams toward the navy. Join these 2 sections to the block section. Press seams away from the blocks.

4. Stitch the vertical stripe sections that go above and below the block section. Press the seams toward the navy fabric.

5. Join the 3 final horizontal sections—top, middle, and bottom (Fig. 2). Press seams away from the blocks.

6. To piece the backing, cut the 5 yard length of backing fabric into 2 lengths, remove the selvages, and join the long edges.

Finish It: For detailed, step-by-step finishing information, including ideas for alternate backings, choosing batting, layering and basting the quilt sandwich, machine quilting options and binding, please refer to "A Patchwork Primer" in my first book, *For Keeps: Meaningful Patchwork for Everyday Living* (2015, Lucky Spool Media).

FULL SCALE

Who says you can't make a king-sized quilt from 6 twelve inch blocks? Not only can it be done, but it can be done in a big, bold, beautiful fashion. Indeed, this isn't your grandma's sampler (or maybe it is, if your grandma is really cool). Your quilt blocks will veritably sing for joy in these weighty frames, strung on musical staff inspired stripes. However you choose to interpret this playful design, it's sure to bring down the house!

Quilted by Amy Wade

Finished Size: 96" x 120"

INGREDIENTS

FOR THE QUILT TOP

6 of your favorite 12 inch blocks

White solid: 5¾ yards

6 Solids of choice: ⅝ yard each

FOR THE QUILT BACK

8½ yards

FOR THE BINDING

⅞ yard

CUTTING

WHITE FABRIC

(24) 8½" x WOF strips

FROM EACH OF 6 SOLID FABRICS

(4) 4½" x WOF strips
   set 2 strips aside
   subcut remaining 2
   strips into (2) 12½"
   lengths, and (2) 20½"
   lengths

BINDING FABRIC

(11) 2½" x WOF strips

MAKE IT

1. Stitch the 12½" x 4½" solid colored strips to either side of the quilt blocks. Press toward the solid fabric. Stitch the 20½" x 4½" solid colored strips to the top and bottom of the quilt block. Press the seams toward the solid fabric. (Fig. 1)

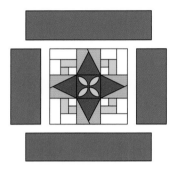

Figure 1

2. Trim the selvages from all the white strips and stitch them into pairs, end to end. You will have 12 extra-long strips of the white.

3. Trim selvages from all the solid colored strips, then cut in half one strip from each of the 6 colors, creating 2 medium length strips. Stitch these medium length strips to both ends of the other like-colored solid colored strip.

Piecing Tip

Sometimes aesthetics trump efficiency. Stitching two seams in the extra-long colored strips (Step 3), instead of one seam, will keep seams from landing right next to one another in these strip sets, and as a result, will make them less noticeable.

4. Using all the extra-long strips, stitch them together along the long edges in groups of 3, creating 6 strip sets of a white-color-white combination. Press the seams toward the colored strips.

5. Subcut the strip sets into the following 2 lengths per color, and discard the remainder:

> top stripe (dark teal): 62½" and 14½"
>
> second stripe from top (orange): 34½" and 42½"
>
> third stripe from the top (green): 3½" and 73½"
>
> third stripe from the bottom (medium teal): 26¼" and 50¾"
>
> second stripe from the bottom (purple): 70¾" and 6¼"
>
> bottom stripe (pink): 14½" and 62½"

Cutting Tip

Check out "By & Large" (see page 127) for helpful ideas on tackling super-sized cutting.

6. Referencing Figure 1, stitch a strip set to all four sides of each framed block.

7. Stitch the 6 rows together (Fig. 2). Press. Trim the sides of the quilt as needed.

8. To piece the backing, cut the 8½ yard length of backing fabric into (3) 102 inch lengths, remove the selvages, and join the long edges.

Finish It: For detailed, step-by-step finishing information, including ideas for alternate backings, choosing batting, layering and basting the quilt sandwich, machine quilting options and binding, please refer to "A Patchwork Primer" in my first book, *For Keeps: Meaningful Patchwork for Everyday Living* (2015, Lucky Spool Media).

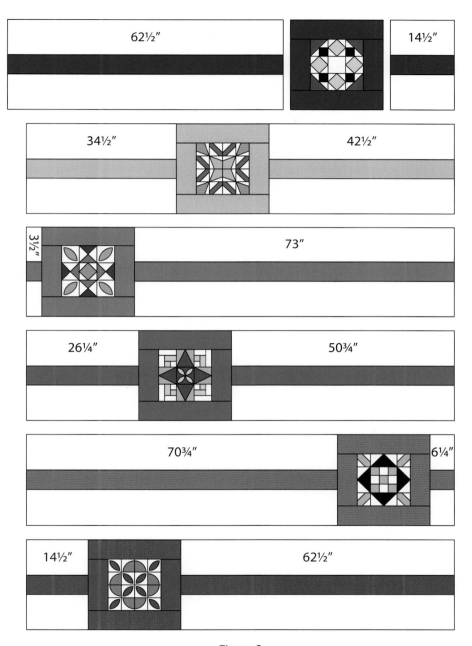

Figure 2

SPOOLS RUSH IN

There's a certain kind of magic that happens when sampler blocks get plugged into a larger overall design. Somehow, the dynamic of the quilt changes, and the blocks take on a new, almost supportive role. This quilt is a perfect example of that magic. The blocks still shine in and of themselves, but set in these giant 24 inch spools, they suddenly become interactive players in the story that is a quilt top. For a cohesive quilt with bold, defined spools, choose spool colors that blend with and complement the colors of each sampler block, and also that contrast well with whatever you choose for a background color. I think you'll agree, that when it comes to pairing your treasured quilt blocks with whimsical oversized spools in your favorite colors (that happen to stitch up ridiculously quickly), a quilter can't help falling in love!

Finished Size:
96" square

INGREDIENTS

FOR THE QUILT TOP
16 of your favorite
12 inch blocks

Gray solid: 3½ yards

16 Solids of choice:
¼ yard each
In my quilt, I used 14 different solids, and repeated 2 of them.

FOR THE QUILT BACK
8½ yards

FOR THE BINDING
¾ yard

CUTTING

GRAY FABRIC
(6) 7" x WOF strips
subcut into (32) 7" squares
(6) 12½" x WOF strips
subcut into (32) 12½" x 6½" rectangles

FROM EACH OF 16 SOLID FABRICS
(1) 7" x WOF strip
subcut into (2) 7" squares, followed by (2) 6½" x 12½" rectangles

BINDING FABRIC
(10) 2½" x WOF strips

Quilted by Amy Wade

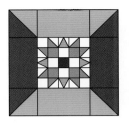 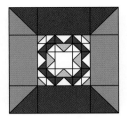 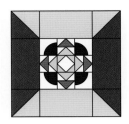 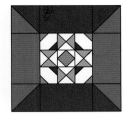

Figure 1

MAKE IT

1. Using all of the 7" squares, stitch a total of 64 HST units (see page 155), 4 per color. Trim the units to 6½" square.

2. Assemble 16 spool blocks in rows of 3 (Fig. 1). Press seams away from the pieced block.

3. Stitch 4 rows of 4 spool blocks each, alternating the block direction, and pressing seams in alternating directions. Stitch the rows together, taking care to pin at each seam intersection. Press.

4. To piece the backing, cut the 8½ yard length of backing fabric into (3) 102 inch lengths, remove the selvages and join the long edges.

Finish It: For detailed, step-by-step finishing information, including ideas for alternate backings, choosing batting, layering and basting the quilt sandwich, machine quilting options and binding, please refer to "A Patchwork Primer" in my other title, *For Keeps: Meaningful Patchwork for Everyday Living* (2015, Lucky Spool Media).

CELESTIAL

We talk about "negative space" a lot in the design world, and I've always thought the term to be a bit of an ironic one. The word "negative", of course, refers to the lack of items in the space around a subject, and yet, this absence is exactly the thing that so often enables the subject to shine at its brightest. In a way, the result of negative space is more positive than anything else. Just like stars in the night sky really seem to twinkle and shine most when they're spaced out a bit, quilt blocks also benefit from some breathing room, and that's the intention behind this quilt. When I scatter my blocks across a blank white canvas, or a sky if you will, with nothing touching any of their 4 sides, they float, they sparkle, they dance.

Quilted by Susan Santistevan

Finished Size:
84" square

INGREDIENTS

FOR THE QUILT TOP
12 of your favorite 12 inch blocks
White fabric: 4¼ yards

FOR THE QUILT BACK
5 yards

FOR THE BINDING
¾ yard

CUTTING
WHITE FABRIC
(12) 12½" x WOF strips
subcut into the following:
(6) 12½" squares
(4) 24½" x 12½" rectangles
(6) 36½" x 12½" rectangles
(1) 60½" x 12½" rectangle (pieced from strips)

Cutting Tip: Check out "By & Large" (see page 127) for helpful ideas on tackling super-sized cutting.

BINDING FABRIC
(9) 2½" x WOF strips

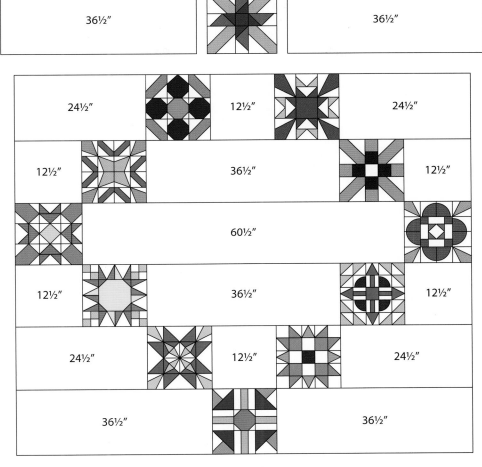

Figure 1

MAKE IT

1. Referencing Figure 1, stitch the blocks, white squares and rectangles into 7 rows. Press the seams toward the white.

2. Join the rows, matching and pinning seam intersections, as well as the lengths between the seams. Press.

3. To piece the backing, cut the 5 yard length of backing fabric into (2) 90" lengths, remove the selvages and join the long edges.

Finish It: For detailed, step-by-step finishing information, including ideas for alternate backings, choosing batting, layering and basting the quilt sandwich, machine quilting options and binding, please refer to "A Patchwork Primer" in my first book, *For Keeps: Meaningful Patchwork for Everyday Living* (2015, Lucky Spool Media).

PRINCESS CUT

A quilt block can be so many things, depending on its surroundings. In this book we've made them into window panes, musical notes, spools, and even stars in an open sky. This quilt plays with the idea of taking a block and setting it in a piece of jewelry, as one would a precious stone. The piecing is quick and easy, but the impact is anything but slight. HSTs in your favorite like-colored prints create bold, glittering stripes, bejeweled with an array of fabulous sampler blocks. Whether you fancy ruby, emerald, or topaz, or prefer to stick to the neutral elegance of pearls and diamonds, your blocks will sparkle in this scrappy quilt!

Finished Size: 72" x 84"

INGREDIENTS

FOR THE QUILT TOP

11 of your favorite 12" blocks

Natural linen fabric: 2⅜ yards

White fabric: 1⅛ yard

Assorted green prints: ⅜ yard (or a fat quarter) of each
Choose 3-6 prints

Assorted pink prints: ⅜ yard (or a fat quarter) of each
Choose 6-11 prints

Assorted blue prints: ⅜ yard (or a fat quarter) of each
Choose 2-4 prints

Tip: For a scrappier looking quilt, choose the maximum number of prints in each color group. Note that each square of print fabric will yield 2 HSTs, so the more prints you choose to incorporate, the more extra (unused) blocks you will end up with. These would be fabulous pieced into the backing, or save them for another quick project!

FOR THE QUILT BACK
5 yards

FOR THE BINDING
⅝ yard

Quilted by Susan Santistevan

CUTTING

ASSORTED GREEN PRINT FABRICS

(3-6) 13" squares

ASSORTED PINK PRINT FABRICS

(6-11) 13" squares

ASSORTED BLUE FABRICS

(2-4) 13" squares

LINEN FABRIC

(1) 12½" square

(21) 13" squares*

This number needs to be the same as the total number of print squares used. For the scrappiest quilt, with no print repeats, 21 squares will be needed. As few as 3 greens, 6 pinks, and 2 blues may be used, making 11 the minimum number of linen squares required.

(4) 8"x WOF strips

subcut into (18) 8" squares

WHITE FABRIC

(3) 12½" x WOF strips

subcut into (9) 12½" squares

BINDING FABRIC

(8) 2½" x WOF strips

MAKE IT

1. Pair each print square with a 13" linen square, and use the drawn-line method to create HST (see page 155) blocks. Each pair will yield 2 blocks. Press and trim to 12½". If you use more than the minimum number of prints, choose 6 green blocks, 11 pink blocks, and 4 blue blocks to use in the quilt. Set the rest aside for the backing or another project.

2. Use the white squares and 8" linen squares to create 9 diagonal stripe blocks (see page 151). Press.

3. Arrange all of the HST, diagonal stripe, and sampler blocks. Stitch into 7 rows of 6 blocks each (Fig. 1, see page 138), alternating the directions when pressing the seams. Stitch rows together. Take care to pin at each seam intersection. Press.

4. To piece the backing, cut the 5 yard length of backing fabric into (2) 90" lengths. Remove the selvage edges and join the long edges.

Finish It: For detailed, step-by-step finishing information, including ideas for alternate backings, choosing batting, layering and basting the quilt sandwich, machine quilting options and binding, please refer to "A Patchwork Primer" in my first book, *For Keeps: Meaningful Patchwork for Everyday Living* (2015, Lucky Spool Media).

Figure 1

BOUNCE

I shared an image of this design with a friend, after telling her I was working on a sampler for a book, and the first words out of her mouth were, "That is NOT what I was expecting!" And it isn't, right? When we think of sampler quilts, I think a lot of us envision a sea of small vintage style blocks in reproduction fabrics, or pristine red and white stars set on point, or we might even think of online block of the month programs or guild swaps. But I'm not sure that a digital audio mixing board typically comes to mind. Well, I'm here to tell you that samplers come in all shapes, sizes, and layouts and they can tell all sorts of stories. This one happens to be a gift for my brother, the music producer and audio engineer. Feel like dancing? Find the beat and stitch up a Bounce quilt. It's therapeutic! But no matter how you feel or what your story is, I hope you always remember that a quilt—even a sampler quilt—can be anything you want it to be—even a dance beat.

Finished Size:
79½" x 84"

INGREDIENTS

FOR THE QUILT TOP
6 of your favorite 12" blocks

White fabric: 2¼ yards
Aqua fabric: ¾ yard
Navy fabric: ¾ yard
Medium pink fabric: ¾ yard
Yellow fabric: ¾ yard
Dark pink fabric: ¾ yard
Green fabric: ¾ yard

FOR THE QUILT BACK
7½ yards

FOR THE BINDING
⅔ yard

Assembled and quilted by
Gina Blanchard

CUTTING

WHITE FABRIC

(10) 2" x WOF strips
remove selvages, stitch end to end, then subcut into (5) 84½" lengths

(4) 12½" x WOF strips
subcut into (28) 12½" x 4½" rectangles

COLORED FABRICS

(2) 12½" x WOF strips from each color
subcut the following pieces:
Aqua fabric:
(8) 12½" x 4½" rectangles
(1) 12½" square

Navy fabric:
(6) 12½" x 4½" rectangles
(1) 24½" x 12½" rectangle

Medium pink fabric:
(3) 12½" x 4½" rectangles
Stitch the second strip and the remainder of the first strip end to end, then cut a 48½" x 12½" rectangle

Yellow fabric:
(4) 12½" x 4½" rectangles
(1) 36½" x 12½" rectangle

Dark pink fabric:
(2) 12½" x 4½" rectangles
Stitch the second strip and the remainder of the first strip end to end, then cut a 60½" x 12½" rectangle

Green fabric:
(6) 12½" x 4½" rectangles
(1) 24½" x 12½" rectangle
Cutting Tip: *Check out "By & Large" (see page 127) for helpful ideas on tackling super-sized cutting.*

BINDING FABRIC

(9) 2½" x WOF strips

MAKE IT

1. Referring to Figure 1, stitch 6 vertical columns using all of the quilt blocks, 4½" x 12½" white rectangles, and all colored pieces. Press seams toward the colored fabrics and away from the sampler blocks.

2. Join the columns, stitching a length of white sashing between each column. To prevent shifting or stretching of the sashing strips as you add them, fold each strip in half and mark the center point with a pin. Then do the same for the column you'll be stitching it to. Match up these two points with a pin, then pin at each end and work your way across the strip, adding pins every 2"–3". Stitch, removing pins as you go, and press the seam toward the sashing.

3. To piece the backing, cut the 5 yard length of backing fabric into (2) 90" lengths, remove the selvage edges, and join the long edges.

Finish It: For detailed, step-by-step finishing information, including ideas for alternate backings, choosing batting, layering and basting the quilt sandwich, machine quilting options and binding, please refer to "A Patchwork Primer" in my first book, *For Keeps: Meaningful Patchwork for Everyday Living* (2015, Lucky Spool Media).

Tip

Accurately measuring long strips of fabric with a tape measure can be challenging because fabric lies differently than a tape measure. I prefer approaching these situations in a more organic way, by using the fabrics strips themselves as the measuring tape. To do this, simply lay out one of your pressed center columns and gently smooth it out. Then lay the strip along the center of the column in the direction that it will be going. Pin one end of the strip to the edge of the column. Smooth the strip along the column until it's nice and flat, but not stretched. Use fabric scissors to cut the strip at the edge of the column, taking care to make a straight 90-degree cut. Not only can you cut all of the sashing strips for this quilt using this measurement technique, but it can also be used for measuring the sashings and borders for any quilt.

Figure 1

POINT TAKEN

Fact: Some sampler layouts are timeless. Timeless is timeless: meaning it fits into all time periods. It never goes out of style. So why fix what isn't broken? I get your point. And you're right. Sometimes all we need to take a traditional layout into the world of online bees and Instagram hashtags, is to infuse it with a fresh, new spin on fabric choice. For this classic on-point frame-style sampler, I updated the look and infused it with personality by using on-trend low volume print fabrics for my background, instead of a solid color (which is funny, because even the concept of using low volume fabrics—which are print fabrics that read like light solids in black & white photos— is a historic one stemming from a time when necessity required resourcefulness. Alas, old is new once again). One simple change, and the result is a quilt that's still timeless and historic, but that feels fresh and current—a perfect home for my bright happy blocks.

Pieced & quilted by
the author &
Gina Blanchard

*Finished Size:
72" square*

INGREDIENTS

FOR THE QUILT TOP
9 of your favorite 12" blocks

9 Colored fabrics:
½ yard each

18 Low volume fabrics:
½ yard each

FOR THE QUILT BACK
4½ yards

FOR THE BINDING
⅝ yard

CUTTING

COLORED PRINT FABRICS
(2) 9½" squares from each of the 9 colored fabrics
  subcut in half diagonally

LOW VOLUME LIGHT NEUTRAL PRINT FABRICS
(1) 13¼" square from each of the 18 low volume fabrics
  subcut in half diagonally

BINDING FABRIC
(8) 2½" x WOF strips

MAKE IT

1. To add the first frame to the sampler blocks, fold a colored print triangle in half, and mark the center of the longest side by finger pressing. Handle triangles with care, so the raw bias edges don't stretch or distort. Align the center marking of the triangle with the center seam of the sampler block, pin and stitch. Repeat with the second triangle on the opposite side of the sampler block. Note that the outside corners of the triangles (dog ears) will hang off each side of the block and the triangles will overlap in the middle (Fig. 1). Press the seams toward the triangles.

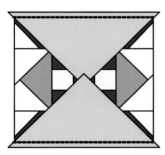

Figure 1

2. Add triangles to the remaining two sides by aligning the centers, pinning, stitching, and pressing toward the triangles (Fig. 2). Trim the excess fabric points (dog ears).

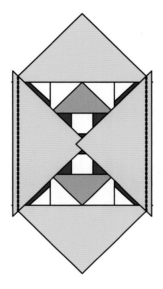

Figure 2

3. Repeat Steps 1-2, using the remaining low volume print triangles to add the outer frame to all 9 sampler blocks. Note that the low volume triangles have been mixed, so that a different print is used on each of the block's 4 sides.

4. Referring to Figure 3 (see page 144). arrange the blocks into a 3x3 pattern and rearrange this until you are pleased with the fabric placements. Stitch the blocks into 3 rows of 3 blocks each. Pin at each seam intersection and press the seams in alternating directions. Stitch the rows together. Press.

5. To piece the backing, cut the 4½ yard length of backing fabric into (2) 81" lengths, remove the selvage edges, and join the long edges. Press.

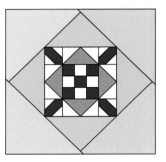
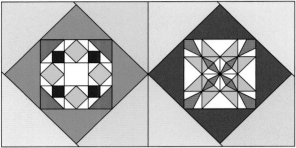

Figure 3

Finish It: For detailed, step-by-step finishing information, including ideas for alternate backings, choosing batting, layering and basting the quilt sandwich, machine quilting options and binding, please refer to "A Patchwork Primer" in my other title, *For Keeps: Meaningful Patchwork for Everyday Living* (2015, Lucky Spool Media).

BEYOND THE SAMPLER:
BLOCK QUILTS TO SINK YOUR TEETH INTO

Even after all those yummy sampler quilts—a taste for nearly every palate—you still might not be in a sampler kind of mood. And that's ok! After 3 years of hosting monthly block-of-the-month programs on my blog, even I needed a break from samplers. But the truth of the matter is, there is SO much more that we can do with quilt blocks.

In this chapter, I want to give you a glimpse of the dynamic, and truly limitless design possibilities that exist when we choose one or two special blocks with which to make an entire quilt. These quilts usually don't have sashing or irregular layouts, so the magic comes from that interaction that happens when the blocks touch one another on all four sides. Patterns that wouldn't typically be evident in a single block or sampler, suddenly start popping out of the woodwork when you put your blocks right next to one another.

DESIGN PLAY

There are many ways to play with one and two block quilt designs and to test drive, if you will,

specific blocks to see what they look like in repeat. Here are a few of my favorite tools and tricks to make design play fun and effective.

SOFTWARE

This is probably one of the most common questions I am asked by quilters—do you use quilt design software, and if so, which one? The answer is yes, I do, and I use it every single day. If you're interested in design play, then I encourage you to explore the market, talk to friends, and read reviews, as there are a myriad quilt design software options available. For all of my designs, I use software developed by the Electric Quilt Company.

Although software may be the most costly of options for design play, averaging around $200 for a program, it's also one of the most efficient and versatile methods. With the ability to draw a block, put it in repeat and insert images of your fabrics with just a few clicks of the button, it can quickly make up for that investment expense, just in the time saved.

SKETCHING BY HAND

This is the way I started out designing my own quilt patterns, and I enjoy going back to it when I have the time, or am away from my computer. Sketching is great because it's fun, it's therapeutic, and it's portable. The downside is that it's more time consuming. Sketching a block or a quilt is one thing, but having to re-draw again and again in order to make adjustments, try out variations, or play with colors, can be another. But if you don't mind the extra time (couldn't we all use a little more artsy time anyway?) and you love to draw, then sketching might just be the perfect design method for you.

Graph paper is essential for accurate scaling. And while most any graph paper will do, the white or light lined options can make it easier to see your work more clearly. My trusty composition book and colored pencils live in the nightstand next to my bed, ready and waiting for an impromptu evening sketch. Most art and craft stores sell a wide variety of colored pencil options, so you can choose the right pencils for you and your budget.

PHOTOS AND PHOTOCOPYING

This is perhaps one of the lesser used (or known) options for design play, but it carries with it some great benefits, and can be used in conjunction with sketching or even blocks you've already sewn. If you have a digital camera and are moderately comfortable with photo-sizing and printing software, then using photos for design might be a fun option for you to explore.

Before my software days, I would stitch a single block, or two or three, or I'd sketch them, and then I would take a tight photo of each block (you could even photograph blocks directly from this book, if you want to start playing with design ideas before you start stitching). I'd then upload the photos to my computer, and print out dozens of copies of the blocks in small sizes (usually around 2-3"), which I cut out with scissors so I could move them around and play with them—almost like a puzzle.

I might alternate blocks in a checkerboard pattern, or see how they look by themselves, or throw a different block in here and there to mix things up. Sometimes, I would even cut the blocks in half or into quarters, and play with those smaller pieces for even more possibilities. I suppose in this day of smart phones and tablets, cutting out paper quilt blocks might seem archaic, but I tell you it is loads of fun (not to mention an incredibly great activity to do with kids), and I think there's something very healthy about getting away from the screen and using your hands whenever possible.

GET INSPIRED

Food and wine magazines tell us over and over again: *You can't have two bold flavors competing.* And they're right! There's no way to ruin a perfectly delicious meal or a fabulous wine, like pairing either with a flavor that fights against it. Delicious foods are best enjoyed with wines that complement them, and vice versa. The same thing applies to pairing quilt blocks. Two perfectly lovely blocks, however glorious on their own, can drown one another out, and turn a would-be stunning quilt into a design that's really difficult to savor and enjoy. The trick is to pair blocks that are different enough from one another so that they aren't competing for your eye.

NEGATIVE SPACE

This is where negative space comes in. We talked about it in the Celestial sampler (see page 134), and the same principles apply here. Negative space, or open spaces in a quilt offer the eye a place to rest and help give definition to a design. Pairing a busy block with a simpler block is an easy way to create this resting place, and to give room for the design to really shine.

FOUR CORNERS

One especially exciting aspect of a 1 or 2 block quilt design is that the corners of the blocks meet, and it's in this 4-corner meeting spot that fun things can happen. This is really where the secondary design repeats blossom, so pay attention to your corners. If you don't like the design you're seeing, consider changing out the corner units, or select a different block. Check out the block combination on page 163 for a great example of a hidden corner gem. Who would have expected white lemons from those two blocks?

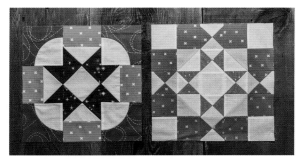

Pairing two busy-looking blocks can create a feeling of chaos.

A perfect pairing gives the eye a place to rest.

CONSTRUCTION TECHNIQUES

All seams in this book, are stitched using a ¼" seam allowance, and with the right sides of the fabrics together.

Many of these units are made using the "stitch & flip" or "drawn line" technique, where a pencil line is draw across the diagonal of the wrong side of a square. The square is then aligned in the corner of another patch, right sides together, and stitched on or ¼" outside the line (depending on the unit). The corner is then trimmed ¼" past the line of stitching to form a seam allowance, and the corner pressed open. While there are a variety of different ways to piece patchwork units, the stitch & flip method offers the advantage of quick and easy cutting, as well as improved accuracy because it side-steps raw biased edges, where other methods call for cut triangles. Because this method is applicable to so many different types of units, it may start to become second nature, and you'll probably find yourself eventually able to skip the unit piecing guide altogether when putting these blocks together.

Draw...

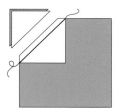

Stitch...

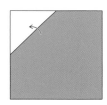

and Flip

UNIT PIECING GUIDE: A-Z

CORNER STRIPE

These units come together in log-cabin fashion, starting with the innermost square, then adding adjacent patches to build the block outward. They can be pieced using individual cuts of fabric, per the cutting instructions in this book; however some prefer a using strips that are at least as long as the unit you are attaching it to, stitching, pressing, and then trimming down to the size needed before attaching the next strip.

This introduces a little more fabric waste, but it can create a more percise finished unit.

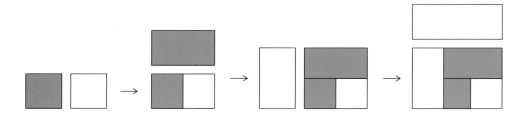

CUT CORNER

This simple unit features a single blunt corner created using the draw, stitch & flip method. Customize the size of the blunt corner by playing with the size ratio between the two squares.

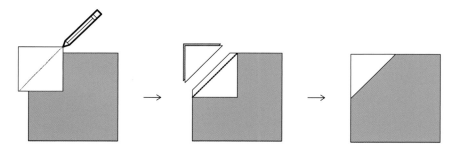

CURVE

Although making these curved units seems challenging at first due to the fabric gathers in the top (concave) piece, the ¼" seam is stitched like any other. With the fabrics right sides together and the wedge shape on the bottom, align and pin the center and outside edge points, then use your fingers to ease the remaining edges together and pin. For a smooth seam, stitch slowly and smooth out any puckers or folds that may develop in the needle's path.

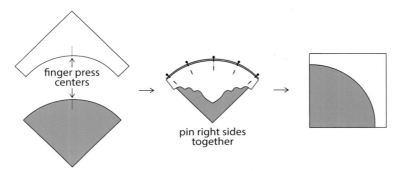

DIAGONAL DIAMOND *from foundation paper pieced triangle units*

To construct this unit, create two pieced triangular sections using the foundation paper piecing method described on page 158, and Template C on page 171. Trim both sections around the perimeter, remove the paper, and stitch them together along the long edge.

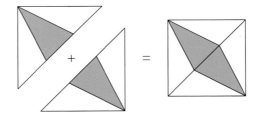

DIAGONAL STRIPE

Use the draw, stitch & flip method on two opposite corners of a square to create a simple, customizable diagonal stripe unit. The larger the corner squares are, in relation to the large square, the narrower the stripe will be.

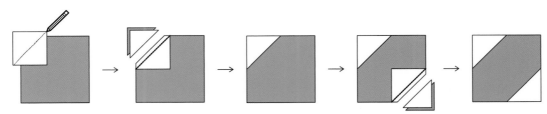

DIAMOND-IN-A-SQUARE

These diamond-in-a-square units begin the same way that the diagonal stripe units do, with draw, stitch & flip patches added to two opposite corners. Press these patches open, then add patches to the remaining two corners. Note that adjacent patches will overlap one another slightly at the ends. These units are easy to make in any size—the cut size of the smaller squares will always be half the finish length of the unit, plus ½".

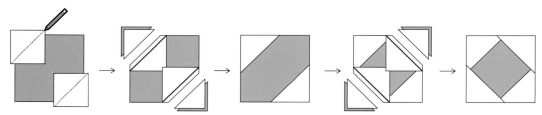

FANCY HALF-SQUARE TRIANGLE (HSTS)

When adding the smaller triangles to the square patch, align the right-angled corners (the pointed tip of the triangle will hang off the edge of the square). Press open before adding each new piece, and press the long seam toward the unpieced half.

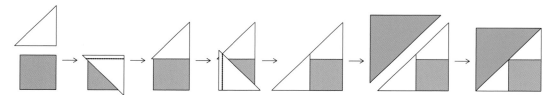

FANCY QUARTER-SQUARE TRIANGLE (QSTS)

Pair a half square rectangle unit with a half-square triangle unit, right sides together with the units aligned exactly as shown. Mark a diagonal line on the wrong side of the top unit (from the top right corner to the bottom left). Stitch on the marked line and trim ¼" from the seam. Discard the excess and press the unit open.

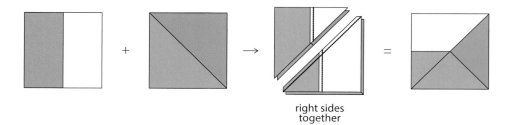

right sides
together

FLYING GEESE

These patchwork essentials are constructed by adding two squares to a rectangle using the draw, stitch & flip method. Press the first triangle open before adding the second square, and be sure the drawn lines are perpendicular to one another. Flying geese are easy to construct in any size—the finished width of the unit is always double the finished height. Add ½" to each of these dimensions to determine the cut size of the rectangle. The two squares will always be cut at the same measurement as the cut height of the rectangle.

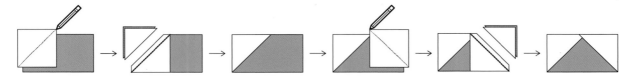

FOUR-PATCH

Whip up simple four-patch units by stitching squares into pairs. Position the 2-patch units right sides together and insert a pin at the seam intersection. Take care to press seams in opposite directions prior to joining the rows.

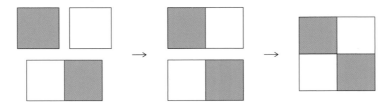

HALF-DIAGONAL DIAMOND

This unit is constructed in exactly the same way as the diagonal diamond unit (see page 151), except that there is an unpieced triangle in place of one of the diagonal diamonds. Refer to the foundation paper piecing instructions on page 158, as well as Template C on page 171.

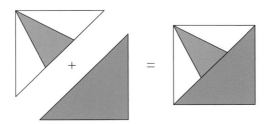

HALF-QUARTER-SQUARE TRIANGLE (HALF-QST)

These units pair a half square triangle (see page 155) with an unpieced square to create the look of a half-square/quarter-square triangle combination. Start by constructing a pair of half-square triangle units, right sides together, with a drawn diagonal line on the wrong side of the top square. Stitch a ¼" seam on both sides of the line then cut the unit in half on the drawn line. Press the two resulting half-square triangle units open, but do not trim. In the same way, pair each of these units with an unpieced square of the same size, with a drawn diagonal line on the wrong side of the unpieced square, perpendicular to the seam. Again, stitch on both sides of the seam, cut the units in half, and press. This process will yield four units (two mirror-image pairs). Trim the units to size.

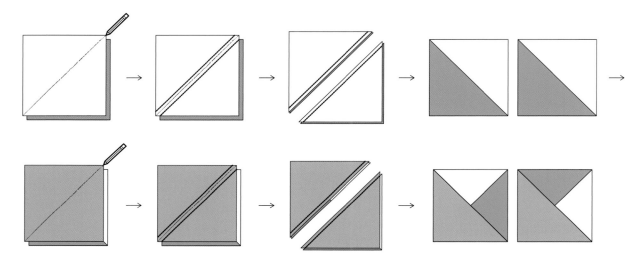

HALF-SQUARE RECTANGLE (HSRS)

Half-square rectangle units are just about as simple and straightforward as can be. If you're making more than one, chain piece them one after the other without clipping threads for a super quick construction process.

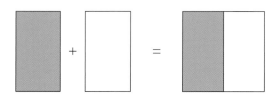

HALF-SQUARE TRIANGLE (HSTS)

A foundational unit in patchwork, half-square triangles can inspire a whole block in and of themselves. This method yields two units. Start with two same-sized squares, right sides together, with a drawn diagonal line on the wrong side of the top square. Stitch a ¼" seam on both sides of the line then cut the unit in half on the drawn line. Press the two resulting half-square triangle units open and trim to size.

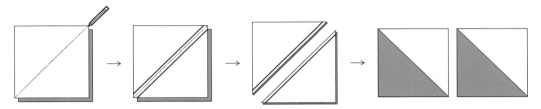

NINE-PATCH

Oldie but a goodie! The 9-patch works well in many different blocks, but also looks great in a quilt all on its own. Stitch your nine squares into three rows of three squares each, pressing seams toward the darker fabric (if both of your fabrics are dark, press the seams in opposite directions by row). Pin at seam intersections, stitch the rows together and press.

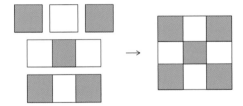

PARTIAL DIAMOND-IN-A-SQUARE

A diamond-in-a-square unit (see page 152) minus one corner patch offers some really interesting possibilities. Play up that unique blunt corner in your design for an eye-catching block.

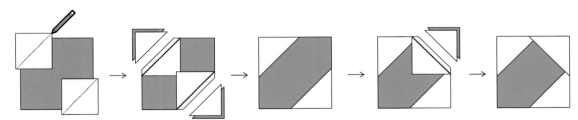

PLUS SIGN

These little plus sign units are a great way to add a modern feel to a block. They're quick and easy to make, and let's face it—just plain cute. Stitch the first and third rows togeteher as you would the 9-patch (see page 155). Replace the second row with a rectangle, join the three rows together and press seams toward the darker fabric.

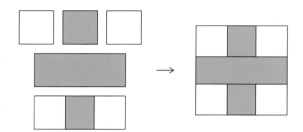

QUARTER-SQUARE TRIANGLE (QSTS)

Another quilt-making basic, these units are quick and easy to make using the draw, stitch & flip method (see page 149). Stitch a pair of squares together as you would the half-square triangle (see page 155). Press the two resulting half-square triangle units open but don't trim yet. Arrange the pair right sides together, so that like colors are opposite one another and the seams are parallel. Repeat the process by drawing a diagonal line on the wrong side of the top unit, perpendicular to the seam. Stitch on both sides, and cut in half on the drawn line. Press and trim the units to size.

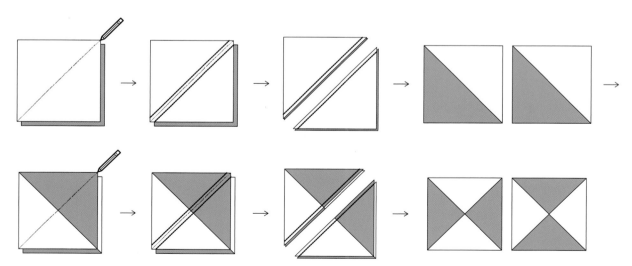

SNOWBALL

These snowball units are just like the diamond-in-a-squares (see page 152), with a square added at each corner and attached using the draw, stitch & flip method (see page 149); however, in this unit, the corner squares are smaller than the large square (so the edges do not overlap). Playing with the size of your smaller squares can yield different looks from this unit.

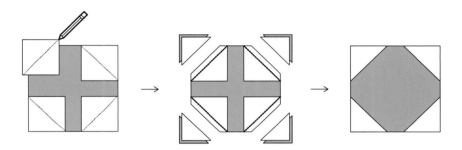

STRIPE

Simple to construct, but definitely not lacking in impact, these striped units can add a bold look to your block. Attach same sized rectangles to one another along their long side. Chain piece when you need to make groups of them, and be sure to press seams toward the darker fabric.

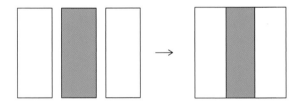

FOUNDATION PAPER PIECING

1. To make a template, draw a 6½" square on a piece of 20 lb. paper and center a 6" square inside that. From the lower left corner of the inner square, draw 4 lines using Figure 1 as a reference. Number each section (Fig. 1). Make sure that you have at least ¼" of fabric extending past the drawn lines.

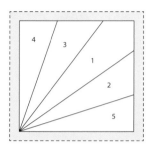

Figure 1

2. Cut your fabric a little bigger than you normally would for machine piecing. Beginning with Section 1, pin your fabric to the wrong side of the template, leaving at least ¼" of fabric extending past the drawn lines. The right side of the fabric should be facing up. (Fig. 2)

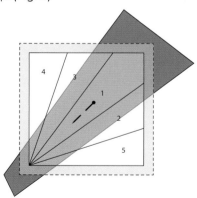

Figure 2

3. After ensuring that your fabric selection for Section 2 also has at least ¼" around all sides (hold the layers up to a sunny window to check), place the fabric for Section 2 on top of the fabric for Section 1, right sides together. Pin in place if needed. Flip over your template so that the numbers are facing you and the fabric is on the bottom.

4. Set your machine's stitch length to 1.8 mm. This will make removing the template paper a lot easier. Sew along the line between Sections 1 and 2, extending into the seam allowance.

5. Fold the paper along the sewn line so that the right sides of the paper are facing. Use a ruler to measure ¼" away from the sewn line onto the exposed fabric. Trim off the excess fabric with a rotary cutter and press open.

6. Repeat for all sections of the template, working in numerical order. (Fig. 3)

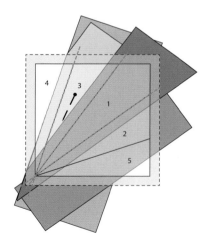

Figure 3

7. Press all seams again, this time on the right side of the fabric. (Fig. 4)

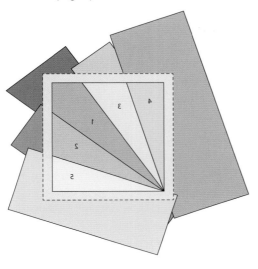

Figure 4

8. With the paper side facing up, trim around the template. Make sure to include any marked seam allowances. (Fig. 5)

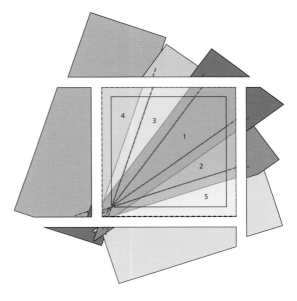

Figure 5

Be sure to trim the block to the finished size prior to piecing these units into rows!

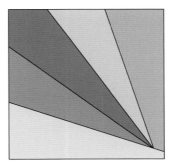

Finished block

A Look at Seam Pressing Strategies

Although the patterns in this book do offer some pressing recommendations, overall, seam pressing is a matter of personal preference. Some quilters always press their seams to the side, some always press them open, and some do a variety of both. Here are a few pressing considerations to keep in mind as you construct your blocks:

- Whenever possible, press away from pieced units, and toward plain units to reduce bulk.

- At particularly bulky points (such as where multiple seams intersect), consider pressing seams open.

- Steam from your iron and spray starch help seams to lie as flat as possible.

- When pressing seams to the side, consider whether or not deep colored fabrics in your seam allowance could show through a lighter fabric and be visible on the front of your quilt. If so, press toward the darker fabric.

- Be mindful of seam direction on seams that line up. When seams are pressed to the side, it's easier to match them tightly if they're pressed in opposite directions.

- When pressing a plain seam between two like fabrics (say, a seam in the middle of a sashing or border strip, or a quilt backing), consider pressing it open. An open seam will provide the flattest look, helping to hide this seam.

- Pressing a seam to the side can offer a subtle texture under the fabric toward which you are pressing. So if you want an area to stand out (an example would be the colorful pie shape in a curved block), press towards that area.

APPLIQUÉ

In this book, all of the flower petal shapes are created using fusible appliqué. This is a technique that involves cutting out a piece of fabric into a specific shape, heat bonding it to the surface of the block or quilt with double-sided fusible web, and then securing the appliqué along the raw edges with stitching.

Following the manufacturer's fusible webbing instructions, use an iron to fuse the wrong side of a fabric to the rough side of paper-backed fusible web. From there, a shape may be traced on the paper side of the web, then cut out the appliqué with small pointed appliqué scissors or a small rotary cutter. Although not applicable for the projects in this book, it is worth noting that the image drawn on the paper backing will appear in the final appliqué as a mirror image. Reverse your shape as you draw on the fusible web backing paper, if needed. The petals shapes we use in this book do not need to be reversed because they are symmetrical.

Once the shapes are cut, peel off the paper backing to reveal the thin layer of adhesive. Arrange the shapes as desired on your background fabric, then follow the manufacturer's instructions to permanently fuse the shapes in place.

Stitch around the perimeter of the appliqué with your favorite finishing stitch (see some of the most popular appliqué stitches at right), being sure to secure the raw edges of the appliqué to the background fabric.

Straight stitch

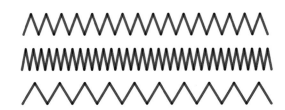

Blind hem stitch

Zig zag stitch in a variety of widths

PERFECT PAIRINGS

Need some inspiration? Here are a few of my favorite combinations. What designs will you dream up? Share your perfect pairings on social media, and remember to tag #TheQuiltBlockCookbook

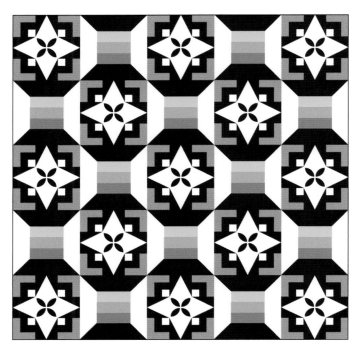

MOON BUG
(page 58)

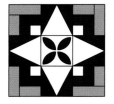

+

UNWIND
(page 78)

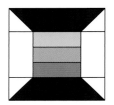

SPIN THE BOTTLE
(page 38)

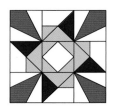

+

ALL AGLOW
(page 122)

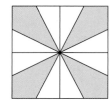

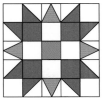 +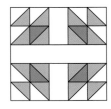

PUMPKIN PIE
(page 82)

WOODED
(page 88)

FIRST KISS
(page 22)

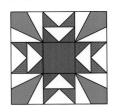 +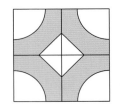

PICCADILLY
(page 104)

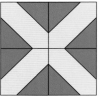
 +
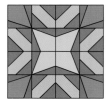

**HOT CROSS
BUN**
(page 120)

DO SI-DO
(page 62)

FLAG DAY
(page 84)

MORE OR LESS
(page 114)

 +
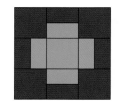

UNIT SIZING CHART

While a variety of methods do exist for making many of these units, note that these cutting dimensions reflect the methods described in this book only, and may or may not be applicable for other methods. Additionally, dimensions for foundation paper piecing, curved piecing, and appliqué units are not included here, as those patches may be cut to size using the Templates on page 166.

All units are square and should be trimmed to the desired unfinished size as needed, except for the flying geese which should be trimmed to the rectangular size listed.

UNIT TYPE	CUTTING DIMENSIONS BY GRID LAYOUT				
	2X2 Finished Size: 6" Unfinished Size: 6½"	**3X3** Finished Size: 4" Unfinished Size: 4½"	**4X4** Finished Size: 3" Unfinished Size: 3½"	**5X5** Finished Size: 2⅜" Unfinished Size: 2⅞"	**6X6** Finished Size: 2" Unfinished Size: 2½"
Corner Stripe	**Background fabric:** (1) 2½" X 6½" (1) 2½" X 4½" (1) 2½" X 2½" **Frame fabric:** (1) 2½" X 4½" (1) 2½" X 2½"	**Background fabric:** (1) 1¾" X 4½" (1) 1¾" X 3¼" (1) 1⅞" X 1⅞" **Frame fabric:** (1) 1⅞" X 3¼" (1) 1⅞" X 1⅞"	**Background fabric:** (1) 1½" X 3 ½" (1) 1½" X 2 ½" (1) 1½" X 1 ½" **Frame fabric:** (1) 1 ½" X 2 ½" (1) 1 ½" X 1 ½"	**Background fabric:** (1) 1⅜" X 2⅞" (1) 1⅜" X 2" (1) 1¼" X 1¼" **Frame fabric:** (1) 1¼" X 2" (1) 1¼" X 1¼"	**Background fabric:** (1) 1¼" X 2 ½" (1) 1¼" X 1¾" (1) 1⅛" X 1⅛" **Frame fabric:** (1) 1⅛" X 1¾" (1) 1⅛" X 1⅛"
Cut Corner	**Center fabric:** (1) 6½" X 6½" **Corner fabric:** (1) 3½" X 3½"	**Center fabric:** (1) 4½" X 4½" **Corner fabric:** (1) 2 ½" X 2½"	**Center fabric:** (1) 3½" X 3½" **Corner fabric:** (1) 2" X 2"	**Center fabric:** (1) 2⅞" X 2⅞" **Corner fabric:** (1) 1¾" X 1¾"	**Center fabric:** (1) 2½" X 2½" **Corner fabric:** (1) 1½" X 1½"
Diamond in a Square	**Center fabric:** (1) 6½" X 6½" **Corner fabric:** (4) 3½" X 3½"	**Center fabric:** (1) 4½" X 4½" **Corner fabric:** (4) 2½" X 2½"	**Center fabric:** (1) 3½" X 3½" **Corner fabric:** (4) 2" X 2"	**Center fabric:** (1) 2⅞" X 2⅞" **Corner fabric:** (4) 1¾" X 1¾"	**Center fabric:** (1) 2½" X 2½" **Corner fabric:** (4) 1½" X 1½"
Partial Diamond in a Square	**Center fabric:** (1) 6½" X 6½" **Corner fabric:** (3) 3½" X 3½"	**Center fabric:** (1) 4½" X 4½" **Corner fabric:** (3) 2½" X 2½"	**Center fabric:** (1) 3½" X 3½" **Corner fabric:** (3) 2" X 2"	**Center fabric:** (1) 2⅞" X 2⅞" **Corner fabric:** (3) 1¾" X 1¾"	**Center fabric:** (1) 2½" X 2½" **Corner fabric:** (3) 1½" X 1½"
Diagonal Stripe Wide *(see block 23)*	**Center fabric:** (1) 6½" X 6½" **Corner fabric:** (2) 3½" X 3½"	**Center fabric:** (1) 4½" X 4½" **Corner fabric:** (2) 2½" X 2½"	**Center fabric:** (1) 3½" X 3½" **Corner fabric:** (2) 2" X 2"	**Center fabric:** (1) 2⅞" X 2⅞" **Corner fabric:** (2) 1¾" X 1¾"	**Center fabric:** (1) 2½" X 2½" **Corner fabric:** (2) 1½" X 1½"

chart continues

UNIT TYPE	CUTTING DIMENSIONS BY GRID LAYOUT				
	2X2 Finished Size: 6" Unfinished Size: 6½"	**3X3** Finished Size: 4" Unfinished Size: 4½"	**4X4** Finished Size: 3" Unfinished Size: 3½"	**5X5** Finished Size: 2⅜" Unfinished Size: 2⅞"	**6X6** Finished Size: 2" Unfinished Size: 2½"
Diagonal Stripe Narrow *(see block 21)*	Center fabric: (1) 6½" X 6½" Corner fabric: (2) 4¼" X 4¼"	Center fabric: (1) 4½" X 4½" Corner fabric: (2) 2⅞" X 2⅞"	Center fabric: (1) 3½" X 3½" Corner fabric: (2) 2¼" X 2¼"	Center fabric: (1) 2⅞" X 2⅞" Corner fabric: (2) 1⅞" X 1⅞"	Center fabric: (1) 2½" X 2½" Corner fabric: (2) 1⅝" X 1⅝"
Fancy Half-Square Triangle	Large triangle fabric: (1) 6⅞" X 6⅞" cut in half diagonally Small triangle fabric: (1) 3⅞" X 3⅞" cut in half diagonally Corner square fabric: (1) 3½" X 3½"	Large triangle fabric: (1) 4⅞" X 4⅞" cut in half diagonally Small triangle fabric: (1) 2⅞" X 2⅞" cut in half diagonally Corner square fabric: (1) 2½" X 2½"	Large triangle fabric: (1) 3⅞" X 3⅞" cut in half diagonally Small triangle fabric: (1) 2⅜" X 2⅜" cut in half diagonally Corner square fabric: (1) 2" X 2"	Large triangle fabric: (1) 3¼" X 3¼" cut in half diagonally Small triangle fabric: (1) 2" X 2" cut in half diagonally Corner square fabric: (1) 1⅝" X 1⅝"	Large triangle fabric: (1) 2⅞" X 2⅞" cut in half diagonally Small triangle fabric: (1) 1⅞" X 1⅞" cut in half diagonally Corner square fabric: (1) 1½" X 1½"
Fancy Quarter-Square Triangle	Background fabric: (1) 6½" X 3½" HST fabric: (1) 6⅞" X 6⅞" HSR fabric: (1) 6½" X 3½" (1) 6⅞" X 6⅞"	Background fabric: (1) 4½" X 2½" HST fabric: (1) 4⅞" X 4⅞" HSR fabric: (1) 4½" X 2½" (1) 4⅞" X 4⅞"	Background fabric: (1) 3½" X 2" HST fabric: (1) 3⅞" X 3⅞" HSR fabric: (1) 3½" X 2" (1) 3⅞" X 3⅞"	Background fabric: (1) 2⅞" X 1¾" HST fabric: (1) 3¼" X 3¼" HSR fabric: (1) 2⅞" X 1¾" (1) 3¼" X 3¼" *Trim HSR units to 2⅞" square.	Background fabric: (1) 2½ X 1½" HST fabric: (1) 2⅞" X 2⅞" HSR fabric: (1) 2½" X 1½" (1) 2⅞" X 2⅞"
Flying Geese	Center fabric: (1) 6½" X 3½" Corner fabric: (2) 3½" X 3½" Unfinished size: 6½" X 3½"	Center fabric: (1) 4½" X 2½" Corner fabric: (2) 2½" X 2½" Unfinished size: 4½" X 2½"	Center fabric: (1) 3½" X 2" Corner fabric: (2) 2" X 2" Unfinished size: 3½" X 2"	Center fabric: (1) 2⅞" X 1¾" Corner fabric: (2) 1¾" X 1¾" Unfinished size: 2⅞" X 1¾"	Center fabric: (1) 2½" X 1½" Corner fabric: (2) 1½" X 1½" Unfinished size: 2½" X 1½"
Four-Patch	From each of two fabrics: (2) 3½" X 3½"	From each of two fabrics: (2) 2½" X 2½"	From each of two fabrics: (2) 2" X 2"	From each of two fabrics: (2) 1¾" X 1¾" *Trim unit to 2⅞".	From each of two fabrics: (2) 1½" X 1½"
Half-Diagonal Diamond	For the unpieced half of the unit: (1) 6⅞" X 6⅞" cut in half diagonally	For the unpieced half of the unit: (1) 4⅞" X 4⅞" cut in half diagonally	For the unpieced half of the unit: (1) 3⅞" X 3⅞" cut in half diagonally	For the unpieced half of the unit: (1) 3¼" X 3¼" cut in half diagonally	For the unpieced half of the unit: (1) 2⅞" X 2⅞" cut in half diagonally

UNIT TYPE	CUTTING DIMENSIONS BY GRID LAYOUT				
	2X2 Finished Size: 6" Unfinished Size: 6½"	**3X3** Finished Size: 4" Unfinished Size: 4½"	**4X4** Finished Size: 3" Unfinished Size: 3½"	**5X5** Finished Size: 2⅜" Unfinished Size: 2⅞"	**6X6** Finished Size: 2" Unfinished Size: 2½"
Half-Quarter-Square Triangle *for 5 x 5 trim unfinished units to 2⅞	From each of two fabrics for the small triangles: (1) 7¼" X 7¼" Large triangle fabric: (1) 6⅞" X 6⅞"	From each of two fabrics for the small triangles: (1) 5¼" X 5¼" Large triangle fabric: (1) 4⅞" X 4⅞"	From each of two fabrics for the small triangles: (1) 4¼" X 4¼" Large triangle fabric: (1) 3⅞" X 3⅞"	From each of two fabrics for the small triangles: (1) 3⅝" X 3⅝" Large triangle fabric: (1) 3⅜" X 3⅜"	From each of two fabrics for the small triangles: (1) 3¼" X 3¼" Large triangle fabric: (1) 2⅞" X 2⅞"
Half-Square Rectangle	From each of two fabrics: (1) 6½" X 3½"	From each of two fabrics: (1) 4½" X 2½"	From each of two fabrics: (1) 3½" X 2"	From each of two fabrics: (1) 2⅞" X 1¾" *Trim unit to 2⅞"	From each of two fabrics: (1) 2½" X 1½"
Half-Square Triangle	From each of two fabrics: (1) 7" X 7"	From each of two fabrics: (1) 5" X 5"	From each of two fabrics: (1) 4" X 4"	From each of two fabrics: (1) 3½" X 3½" *Trim unit to 2⅞".	From each of two fabrics: (1) 3" X 3"
Nine-Patch	Background fabric: (4) 2½" X 2½" Focal fabric: (5) 2½" X 2½"	Background fabric: (4) 1⅞" X 1⅞" Focal fabric: (5) 1⅞" X 1⅞" *Stitch this unit using a seam allowance slightly over ¼".	Background fabric: (4) 1½" X 1½" Focal fabric: (5) 1½" X 1½"	Background fabric: (4) 1¼" X 1¼" Focal fabric: (5) 1¼" X 1¼" *Stitch this unit using a seam allowance slightly under ¼".	Background fabric: (4) 1⅛" X 1⅛" Focal fabric: (5) 1⅛" X 1⅛" *Stitch this unit using a seam allowance slightly under ¼".
Plus Sign	Background fabric: (4) 2½" X 2½" Focal fabric: (2) 2½" X 2½" (1) 2½" X 6½"	Background fabric: (4) 1⅞" X 1⅞" Focal fabric: (2) 1¾" X 1⅞" (1) 1¾" X 4½"	Background fabric: (4) 1½" X 1½" Focal fabric: (2) 1½" X 1½" (1) 1½" X 3½"	Background fabric: (4) 1¼" X 1¼" Focal fabric: (2) 1⅜" X 1¼" (1) 1⅜" X 2⅞"	Background fabric: (4) 1⅛" X 1⅛" Focal fabric: (2) 1¼" X 1⅛" (1) 1¼" X 2½"
Quarter-Square Triangle	From each of two fabrics: (1) 7¼" X 7¼"	From each of two fabrics: (1) 5¼" X 5¼"	From each of two fabrics: (1) 4¼" X 4¼"	From each of two fabrics: (1) 3⅝" X 3⅝"	From each of two fabrics: (1) 3¼" X 3¼"
Snowball	Center fabric: (1) 6½" 6½" Corner fabric: (4) 2¾" X 2¾"	Center fabric: (1) 4½" X 4½" Corner fabric: (4) 1⅞" X 1⅞"	Center fabric: (1) 3½" X 3½" Corner fabric: (4) 1½" X 1½"	Center fabric: (1) 2⅞" X 2⅞" Corner fabric: (4) 1¼" X 1¼"	Center fabric: (1) 2½" X 2½" Corner fabric: (4) 1" X 1"
Stripe	Background fabric: (2) 2½" X 6½" Focal fabric: (1) 2½" X 6½"	Background fabric: (2) 1⅞" X 4½" Focal fabric: (1) 1¾" X 4½"	Background fabric: (2) 1½" X 3½" Focal fabric: (1) 1½" X 3½"	Background fabric: (2) 1¼" X 2⅞" Focal fabric: (1) 1⅜" X 2⅞"	Background fabric: (2) 1⅛" X 2½" Focal Fabric: (1) 1¼" X 2½"

TEMPLATES

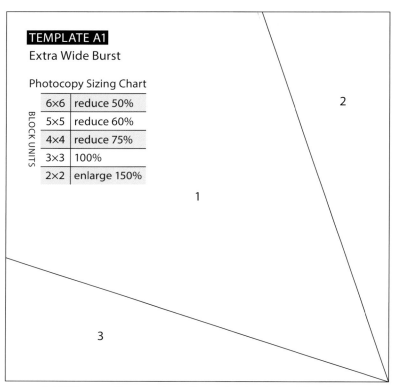

TEMPLATE A1

Extra Wide Burst

Photocopy Sizing Chart

BLOCK UNITS		
6×6	reduce 50%
5×5	reduce 60%
4×4	reduce 75%
3×3	100%
2×2	enlarge 150%

1

2

3

Add ¼" seam allowance to entire perimeter during trimming.

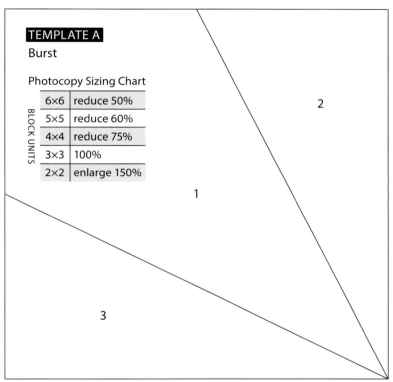

TEMPLATE A
Burst

Photocopy Sizing Chart

BLOCK UNITS		
6×6	reduce 50%
5×5	reduce 60%
4×4	reduce 75%
3×3	100%
2×2	enlarge 150%

1

2

3

Add ¼" seam allowance to entire perimeter during trimming.

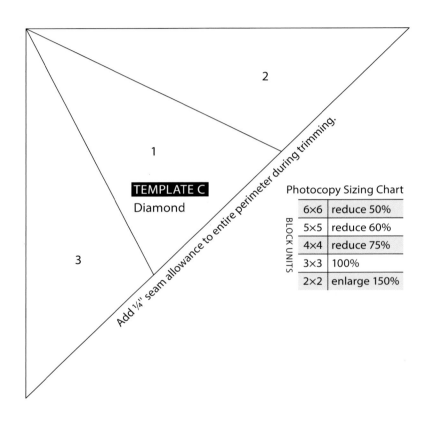

TEMPLATE C
Diamond

2

1

3

Add ¼" seam allowance to entire perimeter during trimming.

Photocopy Sizing Chart

BLOCK UNITS	
6×6	reduce 50%
5×5	reduce 60%
4×4	reduce 75%
3×3	100%
2×2	enlarge 150%

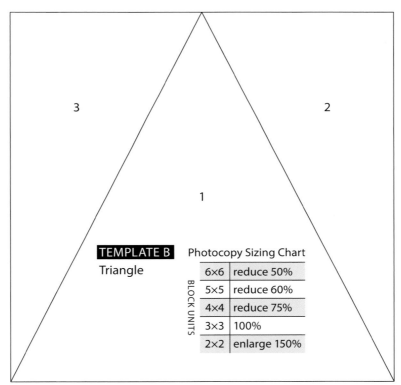

TEMPLATE B
Triangle

3

2

1

Photocopy Sizing Chart

BLOCK UNITS		
6×6	reduce 50%
5×5	reduce 60%
4×4	reduce 75%
3×3	100%
2×2	enlarge 150%

Add ¼" seam allowance to entire perimeter during trimming.

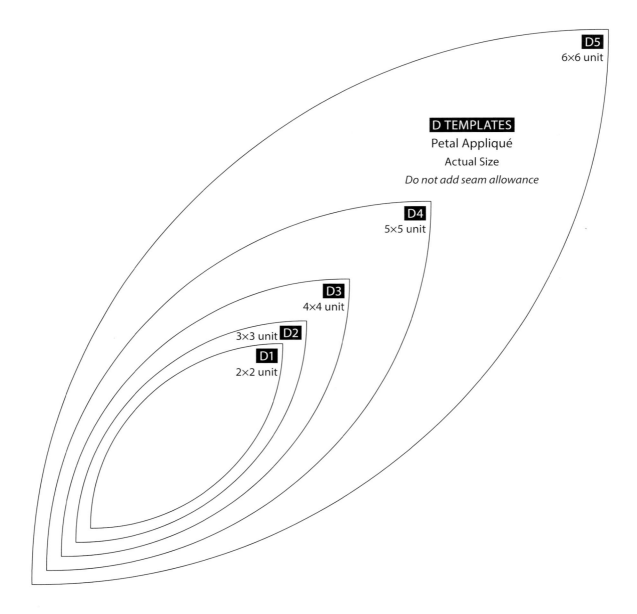

D TEMPLATES

Petal Appliqué

Actual Size

Do not add seam allowance

D5
6×6 unit

D4
5×5 unit

D3
4×4 unit

3×3 unit **D2**

D1
2×2 unit

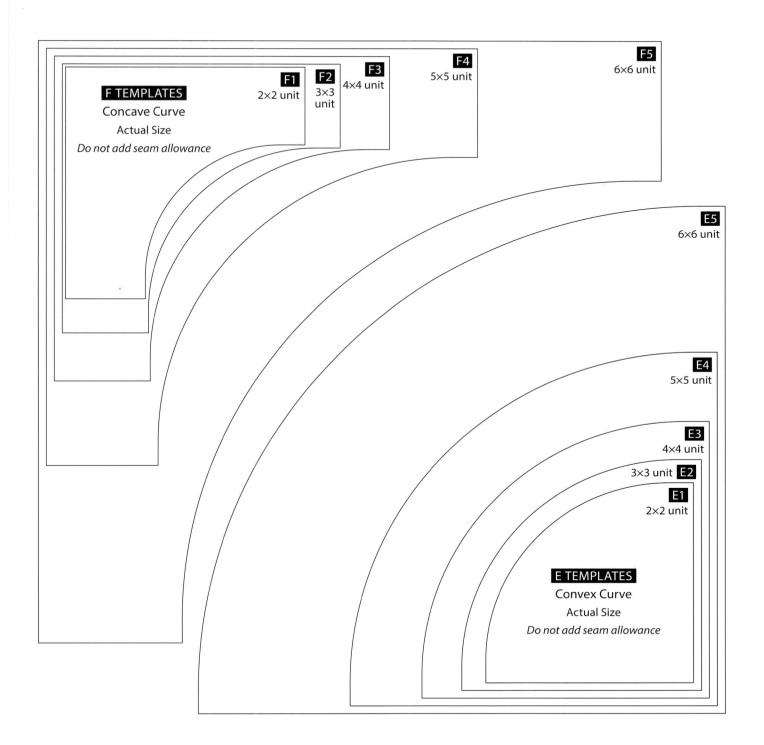

F5
6×6 unit

F1
2×2 unit

F2
3×3 unit

F3
4×4 unit

F4
5×5 unit

F TEMPLATES
Concave Curve
Actual Size
Do not add seam allowance

E5
6×6 unit

E4
5×5 unit

E3
4×4 unit

3×3 unit **E2**

E1
2×2 unit

E TEMPLATES
Convex Curve
Actual Size
Do not add seam allowance

ACKNOWLEDGEMENTS

I'm incredibly grateful to Susanne Woods for her unwavering support. Also thanks to Rae Ann Spitzenberger, Kristy Zacharias, and Nissa Brehmer for bringing these pages to life with design and photography that capture the heart of the book. Thanks to Kari Vojtechovsky, Shea Henderson, and Heather Williamson for their brilliant efforts toward clarity and accuracy. To Susan Guzman for her tireless mentoring and encouragement, and to Angela Pingel and my unquilting brigade for making lemonade. To Amy Wade, Susan Santistevan, Amy Rehnbein and Gina Blanchard for wonderful quilting and piecing help. I couldn't have done this without you. A special thanks to Windham Fabrics, and to Pellon for fabric and batting that is such a joy to work with, and to Fancy Tiger Crafts—the most supportive and inspiring local shop I could ask for. You are a gem. Last, but certainly not least, thanks to my partner in mayhem and magic, Russell, and to the 4 little minions who always make sure I'm up by 6.